FAITH,
FRIENDSHIPS,
AND BUSINESS

HOW FAITH AND FRIENDSHIPS STRENGTHEN YOUR WORK AND PURPOSE

TIANA SANCHEZ WITH:

DESIREE SADDLER - DR. KATIE W. CHU -
BRITTANY EMERY - ARNITA CHAMPION -
TORRIAN SCOTT - LA CREASE COLEMAN –
MARK MAES

PUBLISHING

FAITH, FRIENDSHIPS, AND BUSINESS: How Faith and Friendships Strengthen
Your Work and Purpose
Copyright © 2025 by Tiana Sanchez.

For information contact:
ATG Publishing - info@atgpublishing.com - http://www.atgpublishing.com

ISBN: 9781991123459
First Edition: May 2025
10 9 8 7 6 5 4 3 2 1

ADHD
PUBLISHING STANDARDS
—— LEVEL I ——

CONTENTS

Introduction

In a world divided, where values are tested, and uncertainty is a daily feeling, this book arrives like a well-timed breath of fresh air. Faith, Friendships, and Business is more than a collection of chapters; it is a Godly anointed answer to many prayers. It reminds us that when the world gets loud, we have to get louder. That when the world is our ear, we have to silence it with God's word. That when moral ambiguity sometimes thrives in business, we must return to what grounds us: our faith and our relationships.

This book is for the Faith-filled entrepreneur battling isolation. For the working mom holding down a business and a Bible. For the faith-filled professional navigating boardrooms with conviction and compassion. It's for those who are tired of choosing between their spiritual lives and their professional ambitions—and are ready to integrate both, unapologetically.

Inside these pages, you'll find the voices of real people—leaders, dreamers, and warriors of the faith—who have dared to live out their beliefs in the world of business. Through chapters like *Armor Up with Faith, Bold Moves and Beliefs Matter,* and *Grace-filled Leadership,* these authors unpack how faith is not just a Sunday ritual but a Monday-through-Saturday strategy. You'll read stories of perseverance, forgiveness, decision-making, and ambition—all rooted in biblical truth.

Through chapters like *Living Out Your Values with Faith-Based Decision-Making, Praising God While Dealing with Toxic Relationships,* and *Faithful Ambition,* these authors reveal how godly principles guide not just their personal lives but also their business choices.

You'll discover how staying true to your values—especially when no one is watching—can be your greatest leadership asset. You'll witness how praise and peace can coexist even in the midst of workplace conflict. And you'll be inspired by those who pursued bold goals while keeping their identity rooted in Christ. These stories don't preach perfection—they offer perspective, practical wisdom, and a faith-fueled approach to pursuing purpose and success.

I Forgive You, But I Still Have Trauma walks us through the complicated journey of healing while leading. This chapter shows that carrying faith into business means learning to forgive, even when the wounds still ache. It's about leading with empathy while honoring your own growth.

In *Faith as the Foundation of Life and Business*, you'll see what it means to create something that lasts—something not just built by hand, but by hope and prayer. You will see the power of persistent faith taking center stage, reminding us that when we bring our bold prayers into boardrooms, breakthroughs follow. These are not just stories—they are blueprints for courageous living.

Each chapter brings its own rhythm, its own revelation. Together, they echo the timeless truth of James 2:17— "Faith by itself, if it is not accompanied by action, is dead." The authors in this book have dared to put their faith into motion, and in doing so, they've created impact, influence, and lasting change.

Why does this matter now? Because in 2025, it's not enough to be profitable. You must also be purposeful. Consumers care about values. Employees crave integrity. Leaders are being called to something higher than metrics and margins—they're being called to model Kingdom principles in corporate spaces.

And yet, being a faith-driven professional comes with real challenges. There's the fear of judgment. The pressure to compromise values to "fit in." The tension between humility and ambition. But as Matthew 5:14-16 reminds us, "You are the light of the world... let your light shine before others, that they may see your good deeds and glorify your Father in heaven." This book doesn't shy away from the hard parts—it leans into them with honesty, humor, and hope.

It also reminds us that we don't have to do it alone. Ecclesiastes 4:9-10 says, "Two are better than one… if either of them falls down, one can help the other up." Friendships in business are not a luxury—they are a lifeline. When built on mutual trust and faith, they become the very support system that keeps our purpose intact when profits falter.

Anchoring your business in faith isn't a "nice to have"—it's a must-have. It turns difficult decisions into divine direction. It transforms competition into community. It replaces anxiety with assurance. As Proverbs 3:5-6 promises: "Trust in the Lord with all your heart… and He will make your paths straight."

So, whether you're a business owner or business professional, managing a team, or managing life as an entrepreneur, may this book serve as your companion. Let it remind you that faith is your strategy, friendships are your secret weapon, and business is your mission field.

Welcome to the journey. We are with you, holding your hand and praying for you.

— Tiana Sanchez

Armor Up with Faith

Taking the Shield of Faith to SOAR in Life and Business

By Arnita Champion

Life Is a Battlefield

Let's be real. When you hear words like "life is a battlefield," what comes to mind? By the time we reach our 50s and 60s, we've been through enough to understand that life is not a fairy tale. It's a fight. A fight for purpose, for health, for financial stability, for identity. A fight to hold onto our faith when everything around us is shifting. We, as women and men in our 50s and 60s, have learned much on this battlefield. We have tasted the sweetness of dreams realized and endured the bitterness of dreams deferred. We've built families, businesses, careers—sometimes only to see them crumble and start again. We've battled body image, fought through seasons of loneliness, stared down disappointment, and wrestled with regret. We've worn masks to survive and at times stayed silent when we should have roared. But through it all, we've gained a resilience that no textbook or mentor could have taught. We've learned that survival is not enough—we were made to thrive. We've discovered that the scars we carry are not signs of weakness but badges of honor, proof that we stayed in the fight. And now, standing on this battlefield, wiser, stronger, and more determined, we know the truth: Our greatest victories are still ahead.

Success, growth, and faith come with opposition. The moment you step into your calling, challenges rise to meet you. Fear tightens its grip. Doubt whispers, *"You've missed your chance"*. Procrastination convinces you to wait a little longer. Then life throws in financial struggles, broken relationships, self-doubt, and spiritual attacks. The weight of past mistakes and unmet expectations can feel suffocating. You start questioning, *"Is this all there is? Have I run out of time?"*

I know the weight of those questions because I've lived them. Three failed marriages left me wondering if I was worthy of real love. Years of toxic relationships had me molding myself into someone I was never meant to be. I spent 12 years training for the Olympics, only to fall short—again and again. I gave 36 years of my life to a job, only to walk away with no guarantees of what was next. I launched a business, hoping for success, but faced obstacles at every turn. And through it all, I suppressed my pain, convincing myself that maybe I was the problem, that maybe I wasn't enough.

But here's what I know: **Faith is my weapon.**

Ephesians 6:16 reminds us: *"Take up the shield of faith, with which you can extinguish all the flaming arrows of the evil one."* This isn't just poetic imagery; it's a divine strategy. A command. Faith is not passive—it's an aggressive, intentional defense against every obstacle standing between you and your God-given destiny.

For too long, I settled when I was meant to soar. I stayed grounded with the chickens, buzzards, and ducks when I was created to soar with the eagles. And at 60 years young, it finally clicked— **better late than never, but never late is better**. I was made for more. And so are you.

This battlefield isn't just about surviving—it's about taking back everything that life, fear, and doubt tried to steal. It's about realizing that your best years aren't behind you, they are still ahead. **Are you ready to fight?** Then armor up. It's time to walk, run and SOAR by FAITH.

In the next few pages, I will show you that even when I thought I had failed miserably in all aspects of my life, I **SOARED**. What initially appeared to be failures turned out to be crucial moments of refinement, molding me into the woman I was destined to become—

fearfully and wonderfully made. I wouldn't classify it as an "aha" moment, but rather a "WOW" moment—a true Walking on Water experience!

Much like Peter from the Bible, even when it seemed like I was sinking, all I needed to do was reach deep within myself and respond to God's call on my life to COME and SOAR with Him. I have chosen to break it down by an acrostic - Seeking, Overcoming, Achieving, Righteously and Radiantly.

Keep in mind **SOAR** isn't just an acrostic; it's the principle that transformed my life: SOAR is my story. Seeking when I didn't have answers. Overcoming when life broke me. Achieving by walking in obedience, not by chasing applause. And shining Righteously and Radiantly — not for my glory, but so HIS light would radiate through me. This is the thread God stitched into my being from birth. This is my life's message.

BREAKING DOWN SOAR: THE POWER BEHIND EACH PRINCIPLE

S – Seeking: *Intentionally pursuing something beyond yourself. It's the act of looking for wisdom, truth, and direction—not from the world, but from God. It is not a passive wandering but a deliberate chase after wisdom, purpose, and truth.*

To seek is to humble yourself, to recognize that on your own, you don't have all the answers. It's about surrendering personal plans and aligning with God's greater vision.

For individuals in their 50s and 60s, this can mean seeking clarity about their next season, healing from past wounds, or rediscovering a purpose they thought was lost. Seeking requires discipline— prayer, study, reflection—but it also requires action. It's the first and most important step of any transformation.

O – Overcoming: *Conquering the obstacles that try to keep you bound—fear, doubt, regret, procrastination, and limiting beliefs.*

To overcome is to face adversity head-on and refuse to be defined by it. It is more than surviving; it is rising, conquering, and transforming despite setbacks. Overcoming is the ability to push through fear, doubt, and obstacles, emerging stronger, wiser, and unshaken in your faith. It's not about ignoring hardships; but about refusing to be defined by them. It's understanding that every challenge is not a stop sign but a stepping stone toward your destiny.

Many women at this stage in life (including me) feel they've "missed their moment," but that's a lie. Overcoming is realizing that setbacks are set-ups, failures are fine-tuning, and the best version of you is still being refined.

A – Achieving: *To achieve is to bring a vision into reality through faith-*

fueled action.

Achieving is not just about success—it's about sustainable, God-led progress. It's setting goals that align with your faith, taking daily steps forward (even if they are baby steps) and trusting that obedience leads to fruitfulness. Achievement in this stage of life doesn't look like striving for perfection or proving yourself to others—it's about stepping into the calling God has placed on your heart.

True achievement isn't about quick wins or external validation—it's about walking in obedience, taking intentional steps, and stewarding your gifts well. Achievement isn't measured by applause but by impact—how well you align your life with your God-given purpose.

For those in their 50s and 60s, achieving may mean taking charge of their health, launching a business, deepening their faith, or stepping into leadership roles they once shied away from. It's recognizing that you are still becoming and that there is still more ahead.

R – Radiantly & Righteously: *To live radiantly is to shine from the inside out, illuminating the world with the light of your faith, wisdom, and purpose.*

Radiance is not about vanity or external beauty; it is the glow of someone who has been refined by trials, strengthened by faith, and empowered by grace. To live radiantly is to inspire others—not by what you say, but by the undeniable light of God shining through you. Radiance is about confidence, authenticity, and walking boldly in the light of Christ. It means **shining from the inside out**, not for validation but because you are fully aligned with your God-given purpose.

Righteousness isn't about perfection—it's about living in alignment with truth, embracing grace, and leading by example.

To live radiantly and righteously is to no longer shrink, apologize for who you are, or dim your light to make others comfortable. It's walking in faith without hesitation, inspiring others by how you live, and refusing to settle for a life of mediocrity.

These aren't just words—they're declarations! When you seek, overcome, achieve, live righteously, and radiate, you're walking in unstoppable purpose.

Each of these words builds upon the other. **Seeking** brings clarity. **Overcoming** strengthens you. **Achieving** empowers you. **Radiating** allows you to shine without apology. Together, they create a **blueprint for transformation**, ensuring that no matter where you've been, you can still **SOAR**.

Coming up, I will show you how I went from broken to soaring.

How I found strength in what I thought were my weakest moments. And how you, too, can rise above every challenge that tries to hold you back.

What I once saw as roadblocks were actually stepping stones. What I thought were dead ends were detours leading me toward God's greater purpose. I will show you how I went from broken to soaring. How I found strength in what I thought were my weakest moments. And how you, too, can rise above every challenge that tries to hold you back.

Now let's talk about the S in SOAR.

S – Seeking First the Kingdom

Who's Kingdom? God's Kingdom.

Matthew 6:33 declares, *"Seek first the kingdom of God and His righteousness, and all these things will be added to you."* Everything we need—provision, clarity, strength—flows from putting God first. This lesson became clearer than ever when I made the life-altering decision to leave California and move to Texas.

In just thirty days, my home was painted inside and out, decluttered of all unnecessary items, and put on the market for sale. It sold right after the first open house, but when the buyers faced difficulties enrolling their children in the school district, the escrow fell through. I was heartbroken. Anxiety took hold of me, and fear quietly asked, *"What if I lose it all?"* After all, I had already made a deposit on my new home in Texas. Fear shouted, *"Stay still/Don't move,"* while Faith softly urged, *"Keep moving forward."*

It only took me a minute to say to my realtor, *"Put it back on the market."* And just like that, the next weekend, another offer came through, and this time it closed in 30 days. The simultaneous sale of my California home and the purchase of my Texas home happened so seamlessly, I knew it was God's hand at work. What felt like an obstacle was actually divine timing.

Walking by Faith, Not by Sight

Leaving behind everything I had known for decades was terrifying. I had built a life, a career, a home, and yet God was calling me into the unknown. Seeking Him first meant trusting that if He led me to Texas, He would make a way. And He did—flawlessly.

Seeking Him first isn't passive—it's a daily decision. It's choosing obedience over comfort. It's aligning your business, health, and dreams with His will. It's making space for His direction, even when it doesn't make sense.

Faith also became my shield through the brokenness of three divorces. Each marriage carried promises that ultimately ended in brokenness. Don't get me wrong, I take full ownership in each instance, and I am not here to place blame on my former spouses alone—I recognize my own faults.

I placed unreasonable expectations on men who were never designed to validate me, to fill the void only God could fill. I sought love in the arms of people instead of seeking it in the presence of my Creator. It was all because my heart longed for security and stability, but I was building on an unstable foundation.

In my pursuit of love, I also lost myself. I battled a severe eating disorder, shifting my body to fit the expectations of others. I became addicted to approval, sacrificing my health, my identity, and my self-worth to please people. I wore different masks, shaping myself into what I thought others wanted me to be.

In the process, I lost sight of who God created me to be—His daughter, made in His image.

When you seek God first, you find everything else in its rightful place. You no longer seek validation in human relationships. You no longer build your worth on shifting sand. You stand firm, knowing your identity is rooted in Christ.

What would happen if you truly put God first? If you surrendered your plans for His? If you stopped forcing doors open and let Him guide your steps? Everything changes when you seek Him first. The question is—will you?

O – Overcoming Fear, Doubt, and Procrastination

Excuses keep people stuck. Fear tells them they'll fail. Doubt makes them hesitate. Procrastination delays obedience.

The Deepest Battle: Losing and Finding Myself Again

Most people don't know this about me, but I am a three-time U.S. Olympic Trial Finalist in the 100 and 400-meter hurdles, I fervently chased my dream of joining the U.S. Olympic Track and Field Team. Between 1984 and 1996, I faced intense challenges. Each defeat, every setback, and each missed qualification could have led me to give up. However, this journey was about more than just losing races; it was about the possibility of losing a dream that I had dedicated 12 long years to. The countless hours of training, the sacrifices made, the injuries endured, and the mental and emotional fatigue were all part of the struggle. I poured my heart and soul into this pursuit, yet it still felt insufficient.

When I didn't make the US Olympic Team, I felt humiliated, broken, and betrayed by my own efforts. I questioned everything— my talent, my worth, even my faith. I had built my identity around this one goal, believing that if I just worked hard enough, sacrificed enough, and proved myself, then I would finally achieve it. But when it slipped through my fingers time and time again, something inside me shattered.

I felt anger—not just at myself but at God. Hadn't I prayed enough? Hadn't I done everything right? Why did He let me fall short? It felt like He had abandoned me, like He had dangled this dream in front of me only to snatch it away. I wrestled with feelings of failure, questioning if I had wasted 12 years of my life chasing something that was never meant for me.

But here's what I now understand: My loss wasn't a failure—it was a redirection.

For every woman who has spent decades pouring herself into something—a marriage, a career, a dream—only to watch it fall apart, I see you. I know the pain of feeling like you've invested everything into something that didn't work out. Maybe you've given years to a marriage that ended in divorce. Maybe you spent decades in a career that left you unfulfilled. Maybe you've chased a dream, only to come up short, wondering if you ever really had what it takes.

But let me tell you something: You are not defined by what didn't happen. Your worth is not measured by the dream that didn't come to pass. God doesn't waste pain—He repurposes it. Those 12 years weren't a waste; they were a training ground for everything I would do later in life. The discipline, the resilience, the ability to get up after every fall—it all prepared me for a greater purpose, even though I couldn't see it at the time.

If you're in a season where it feels like everything is falling apart, hold on. What feels like a dead end may actually be a divine detour. God is not done with you. The dream may have shifted, but the purpose behind it is still alive. And if you keep moving forward—if you refuse to let the disappointment define you—you will SOAR in ways you never imagined.

Because sometimes, losing what we thought we wanted is the only way to discover what we were truly made for.

Moving Past Fear, Doubt, and Procrastination

When doubt whispers, *"What if you fail?"* Faith declares, *"What if you don't?"* Fear says, *"You're too old, too late, too unqualified."* Faith says, *"God equips the called. Procrastination says, Tomorrow is a better time to start."* Faith says, *"Now is the time."*

I spent years believing the lies that whispered I wasn't enough; I had missed my chance; I was too late; I needed more time, more knowledge, more preparation. But the truth is, doubt and fear don't wait for a convenient time to leave. They linger until you decide to move despite them.

Procrastination nearly kept me from launching my business. I told myself I needed more resources, more experience, more confirmation. I convinced myself that I had to have everything in order before I took the first step. But one day, I heard God ask me: *"Do you trust Me?"*

That question hit me hard. Trust wasn't just about praying; it was about moving. It was about taking action when I couldn't see the outcome. The moment I stepped forward, doors that had been closed began to open. Fear started to loosen its grip. Opportunities appeared. But nothing—absolutely nothing—happened until I made the decision to stop waiting and start moving.

To every woman who has put off a dream, who has delayed stepping into her calling, who has convinced herself she needs just a little more time: **this is your moment.**

You don't need more validation. You don't need a perfect plan. You don't need to wait for the "right time."

The right time is now.

Overcoming isn't about waiting for fear to disappear; it's about choosing to move even when fear is screaming at you to stop. It's about refusing to let past failures define your future. It's about believing that if God called you to it, He will bring you through it.

The battle isn't in the waiting—it's in the decision. Will you keep delaying, or will you take the first step? **Overcoming is a choice.**

I chose to step forward. And I promise you this: when you do the same, you will discover that the strength you thought you lacked was inside you all along. You just had to move to find it.

Confronting the Truth About Self-Image

I also procrastinated when it came to confronting the truth about my self-image. I believed if I just lost a few more pounds, looked a certain way, or molded myself into someone else's ideal, I would be accepted. I thought that if I became "her"—the woman society said I should be—then I would finally be worthy. But acceptance never came because I was seeking it from people who could never offer what I truly needed.

I spent years shaping myself to fit someone else's expectations. I wore different masks for different situations, afraid to show up as my true self. I became obsessed with achieving a certain size, believing that my worth was directly tied to a number on the scale or the approval of others. And when I still felt empty, still felt unseen, I blamed myself. I told myself I just wasn't enough—not pretty enough, not fit enough, not desirable enough.

Does this sound familiar? Have you ever looked in the mirror and felt like no matter what you do, it will never be enough? Have you ever felt like if you could just "fix" one more thing about yourself, then maybe—just maybe—you would finally feel loved? Valued? Whole?

The truth is **you will never find lasting validation in the eyes of the world.** No weight loss, no beauty treatment, no outside approval will ever fill the void that only God can fill. Healing began for me the moment I stopped striving for worldly approval and surrendered to God's love.

God never asked me to shrink myself to be loved. He never asked me to erase the parts of me that made me unique. He never measured my worth by my waistline or my reflection. He called me worthy from the start. And He says the same about you.

No More Waiting. No More Excuses.

What excuses are you making? What fears hold you back? What have you delayed, waiting for the "perfect" moment? Maybe you've put off starting your business because you don't think you're qualified. Maybe you've held back from stepping into your purpose because you're afraid of what people will say. Maybe you've convinced yourself that you'll start taking care of yourself "tomorrow."

But let me tell you something: There is no perfect moment. There is only now.

The world doesn't wait—why should you?

Overcome fear with action. Overcome doubt with faith. Overcome procrastination with obedience. It's time to step forward. It's time to stop trying to fit into the world's version of "enough" and start embracing the version of you that God created.

Because **you were never meant to be small. You were meant to SOAR.**

A – ACHIEVING LASTING AND SUSTAINABLE GOALS

Quick fixes don't last. Faith, health, success—all require commitment.

For years, I believed that success came in big, dramatic moments. I thought transformation meant instant results, that breakthrough happened overnight. But the reality? Achievement is built in the quiet, disciplined, daily choices we make when no one is watching.

After years as an athlete, I knew my body needed care, yet I still made excuses. *"I'm too busy. I'll start next week. Just one more day."* But procrastination led to decline. My energy dropped. My strength faded. I wasn't honoring the body God gave me. I looked in the mirror and didn't recognize the woman staring back at me—not because of age, but because of neglect.

And for years, I hid the truth.

Behind the discipline of an athlete, I was fighting a battle with food. I was obsessed with controlling my weight. Anorexia whispered that if I just ate less, I'd be more worthy. Bulimia promised me that I could consume my emotions, as long as I erased the evidence afterward. Diet pills became my secret weapon, giving me an illusion of control while robbing me of my health. I spent years hiding behind the mask of an athlete, convincing myself that I was "fine." But inside, I was anything but fine.

Then came the wake-up call I couldn't ignore: high blood pressure and cholesterol levels that put me at risk, even as an elite athlete. I was wrecking my body in the pursuit of perfection. I had placed my worth in what I could control, instead of surrendering my body, my health, and my struggles to God.

I had to face the hard truth: I wasn't being a good steward of what God had given me. That realization sparked change. Not because I was chasing a number on the scale, not because I was desperate for approval, but because I was ready for wholeness—physically, mentally, and spiritually.

So, I didn't chase diets or temporary solutions—I built sustainable habits. I moved daily. I nourished my body. I disciplined my mind. I honored my temple. And everything shifted. Not instantly. Not overnight. But little by little, day by day, obedience by obedience, I rebuilt what I had neglected.

The same principle applies to business and faith. Success isn't built overnight. It's the result of consistent, small steps and intentional actions. It's making daily choices that align with your long-term vision.

Faith isn't a one-time decision; it's a lifestyle. It's showing up, even when results aren't immediate. It's trusting God's process, even when you don't see it or understand it.

Are you building something that lasts? Or are you chasing quick wins?

Are you starting over every Monday, making promises you don't keep? Have you given up because you didn't see results fast enough? Are you waiting for motivation instead of building discipline?

Lasting transformation requires daily commitment.

That's what separates those who dream from those who achieve.

So today, I challenge you: Start. Just start. Don't wait for the perfect moment. Don't wait for motivation. Take one step. Make one shift. Because small steps taken in faith will always lead to greater breakthroughs than standing still in doubt.

Your future is built on what you do today. So, what are you waiting for? It's time to achieve what God has already called you to.

R – Radiating and Righteously Living for Christ in Every Area

For years, I thought shining meant standing in the spotlight. I believed that if I could just accomplish enough, impress enough, and prove myself enough, I would be seen. I wanted to shine—but I wanted to shine for me.

And it failed every single time.

I exhausted myself trying to build a platform where my name was known, my talent was praised, and my presence was recognized. But the glow was temporary. The applause always faded. And no matter how brightly I tried to shine, it was never enough. Because the light wasn't mine to begin with.

God doesn't ask us to shine so we can be glorified. He calls us to radiate His light, so that when others see us, they see Him.

The Cost of Running from God's Light

I spent years running—running from surrender, running from obedience, running from the humility it takes to let God be the one in control. I wanted to be in charge of my own radiance, and it took me a lifetime to realize that real light doesn't come from striving—it comes from surrender.

Living radiantly and righteously isn't about performing. It isn't about perfection. It's about being in alignment with God's purpose and allowing Him to use every part of your life—your wins, your wounds, your past, and your purpose—to point back to Him.

It's about walking in truth, integrity, and His divine alignment. Righteousness isn't a performance—it's a posture of faith, a commitment to reflect God's love, and a decision to honor Him in everything we do.

When I finally surrendered, something shifted. I stopped forcing opportunities and started flowing in obedience. I stopped worrying about what people thought and started caring more about what God required of me. And suddenly, I no longer felt like I had to prove my worth - I was already enough in Him.

A Light That Doesn't Dim

Women in their 50s and 60s often feel overlooked, like their best years have passed, like they have lost their glow. But let me tell you something: God's light does not dim with age. The world says you've peaked. The world says it's too late. But the world is wrong.

"Your latter days are greater than the former," (Job 8:7).

"Faith was a radiant lamp unto my feet and a light unto my path" (Psalms 119:105), which led me home. After 60 years of running, I surrendered it all—my fears, my image, my expectations, my heart. I laid down my masks and let God reveal the woman He created me to be.

God doesn't call the qualified—He qualifies the called.

Radiating His glory means stepping up. It means using your gifts. It means showing up fully, unapologetically, without watering yourself down. It means being excellent in business, diligent in health, fearless in faith. It means refusing to dim your light so that others may shine.

To live radiantly is to shine from the inside out, illuminating the world with the light of your faith, wisdom, and purpose. Radiance is not about vanity or external beauty; it is the glow of someone who has been refined by trials, strengthened by faith, and empowered by grace. To live radiantly is to inspire others—not by what you say, but by the undeniable light of God shining through you.

These aren't just words—they're declarations! When you seek, overcome, achieve, live righteously, and radiate, you're walking in unstoppable purpose.

Conclusion: Amor Up with Your Shield of Faith and Move Forward

Faith is more than just a belief—it's a bold decision. Every single day, you stand at a crossroads: Will you trust God, or will you let fear take the reins? Will you step into the calling He has placed on your life, or will you shrink back into comfort?

This is your defining moment.

No more waiting for the "right" time. No more questioning whether you're qualified, ready, or worthy. The same God who strengthened me in the grueling hours of Olympic training, who carried me through heartbreak, who sustained me through setbacks and struggles—that same God is calling YOU forward.

But faith without action is just a wish.

So, I ask you:

Will you **SEEK** Him with unwavering faith, even when the path is unclear?

Will you **OVERCOME** the doubts, the excuses, and the fear of failure?

Will you **ACHIEVE**, not by striving in your own strength, but by stepping into your divine assignment?

Will you **RADIATE** His power and His presence in everything you do?

This is your invitation to SOAR. Not someday. Not when you feel "ready." NOW.

Pick up your shield. Move forward. Walk boldly.

And when you do—watch how God moves in ways you never imagined.

It's time. Go SOAR.

ABOUT ARNITA CHAMPION

Arnita Champion is the definition of faith in motion. From sprinting down Olympic tracks to standing tall on stages of transformation, her journey is a masterclass in turning trials into triumph. A world-class hurdler, Arnita competed in the 1984, 1988, and 1992 U.S. Olympic Trials and  proudly represented Team USA in the 1991 World Championships. But when an injury sidelined her 1996 Olympic dream, she didn't fall—she rose.

What emerged was more than an athlete. It was a woman on a mission. Today, Arnita is a powerhouse motivational speaker, wellness entrepreneur, and spiritual mentor who inspires women across generations to SOAR—Seek, Overcome, Achieve, and Radiantly Righteously Rise.

She's the creator of the SOAR Journals and Affirmation Cards—spiritual growth tools rooted in faith, fitness, food, and fashion—and the founder of C-Bandz, her signature resistance bands designed to help women build strength without fear or injury. Her bestselling book, 6 Secrets to Growing Younger, empowers women to reclaim their energy, purpose, and worth at any stage of life.

Arnita's story is one of reinvention, resilience, and radiant faith. Through divorce, health challenges, and reinvention, she's become a living example of what it means to be Aged by Fire—refined by life's toughest moments, and stronger because of them.

Whether coaching, speaking, or creating tools that change lives, Arnita Champion is equipping women everywhere to armor up, live boldly, and rise faithfully—in business, in wellness, and in purpose.

Faith as the Foundation of Life and Business

By Mark Maes

Life and business are unpredictable journeys—filled with highs and lows, opportunities and challenges, victories and setbacks. No matter how much we plan, prepare, or strategize, we inevitably face moments when we must step into the unknown. And in those moments—when logic, reason, and even experience fall short—**faith becomes the defining factor in how we move forward.**

Faith is not merely a religious belief, or a ritual practiced on Sundays; it is a living, breathing force that influences every aspect of our lives. It shapes our decisions, fuels our perseverance, and gives us the courage to take steps we otherwise might never take. For me, faith has been the learned cornerstone of my journey—not just in my personal life but in my career as a business owner and advisor. It has carried me through loss, failure, uncertainty, and success. Faith has taught me that the greatest breakthroughs often come after the greatest trials—and that God's hand is always at work, even when we can't see it.

I didn't always see faith the way I do now. Raised in a Catholic household, my early understanding of God was rooted in tradition: baptism, first communion, confirmation, and the structured teachings of the church. But as life unfolded, I realized that faith is far more than tradition; it's a deeply personal relationship with God. A relationship built through trust, surrender, and daily seeking. It's one thing to know who God is; it's another to walk in faith and experience His presence in every part of life and business.

Through the trials and victories of my life, I've learned that those who actively seek God's direction approach life and business differently. They make decisions not out of fear, but out of faith. They navigate setbacks with perseverance, not despair. They don't just work for success—they build with purpose.

In this chapter, I want to share the power of faith in decision-making. I'll walk you through key insights that have shaped how I understand faith's influence: how it provides vision, trust, resilience, integrity, purpose, and ultimately, a lasting legacy. My hope is that by the end of this chapter, you won't see faith merely as a concept, but as a verb—an active force that shapes how you live, work, and lead.

Faith is not passive. It's the very foundation on which success is built. When we align our lives and businesses with God's plan, we experience peace, clarity, and fulfillment that no worldly achievement can provide.

My prayer is that as you read these words, you'll be encouraged to seek God more deeply, trust Him more fully, and walk in faith with unwavering confidence.

Let's begin.

THE CORNERSTONE OF FAITH – A JOURNEY OF TRUST AND PURPOSE

Life and business are anything but predictable. We set goals, create strategies, and plan for success, yet time and again we find ourselves facing unexpected twists and turns. The question is not whether we will encounter uncertainty—it's how we'll navigate it. And the answer, I've learned, is faith.

Faith isn't passive belief; it's the very foundation on which we build our lives and businesses. It's the trust that even when we don't have all the answers, God does. It's the confidence that even when circumstances appear chaotic, there is a divine order at work. Without faith, we're left relying solely on our limited understanding—

shaped by our past, our environment, our experience.

But faith allows us to rise above those limits and step into something greater: God's purpose.

I remember a season of business growth when suddenly, everything seemed to unravel. Despite years of effort, long hours, and strategic planning, things were falling apart. Trust and loyalty were eroding. Doubt crept in.

I questioned whether I was on the right path, whether I'd made the right decisions. But in those moments of doubt, one scripture anchored me:

"Trust in the Lord with all your heart and lean not on your own understanding; in all your ways submit to Him, and He will make your paths straight." - Proverbs 3:5-6

Without faith, failure feels like the end of the road. With faith, failure becomes a lesson, a redirection, a refining process. It's in those tests that testimonies are born, where our beliefs are shaped and strengthened. Inexperience and immaturity resist this, but over time, experience teaches us to embrace and even capitalize on challenges.

THE LIARS CLUB – LESSONS FROM BETRAYAL AND GOD'S GREATER PROMISE

In business, you expect challenges. You expect competition, mistakes, and even loss. But betrayal—especially from someone you love like family—**cuts deeper than anything numbers can measure.**

We once had a Director of Operations who, to this day, remains the smoothest, most gifted liar I've ever met. After decades in the construction industry, having seen every kind of operator you can imagine, nothing prepared me for him. He was a family member of a large construction company we worked with, eager to make a name for himself outside his family's shadow. I saw potential and opened doors for him that should have taken years to open.

At first, everything seemed promising. Fast accomplishments. Smooth talk. The appearance of success. But soon, cracks appeared, and we saw excuses tied to marital problems, family dysfunction, pressures at home. I responded with compassion. We paid for private and couples counseling. We gave him time off to invest in his family, to heal. We stood beside him.

Only to discover it was all a lie.

He was stealing. Misappropriating labor. Falsifying invoices.

Charging personal expenses to company accounts. It broke my heart—not because of the money, but because I loved him like a son. I thought I was lifting him up. But when I looked up, I realized he wasn't reaching for me—he was standing on my head, pushing me deeper, and he didn't care.

That kind of betrayal tests a man's soul.

Everything in me felt justified to retaliate, to destroy his reputation. Truthfully, in the moment, I felt qualified to do so. But I knew that wasn't God's way. No matter how right I felt in my flesh, I knew vengeance wasn't mine to take. I waited. I surrendered my anger to God.

Six months later, another trusted employee betrayed me similarly. It knocked the wind out of me. It wasn't just about the money—it was the shattering realization that what I thought was family had been a facade.

I'd given my heart, my best—and it still wasn't enough to protect what mattered. In that deep place of brokenness, beyond anger and disappointment, I cried out: *"Why, Lord? Why? How do I keep going?"*

And it was there, in surrender—not demanding answers, but yielding—that I finally heard Him. I wasn't asking anymore; I was listening.

That's when I learned: when we seek God with total anticipation, belief, and love—not casually, but desperately, expectantly—He reveals Himself in undeniable ways.

The Bible isn't a storybook or a rulebook. It's a living, breathing promise. An invitation to a relationship so merciful, so real, it defies logic and dismantles every lie we've believed.

We think we don't deserve it. We think it's not for us. We disqualify ourselves. But how wrong we are.

It's not your fault if you didn't know. But now you do—and now it's your opportunity.

For me, this unshakable truth of God's faithfulness was forged in the fire of betrayal, heartache, and surrender.

To God be the glory. Always. But letting go and letting God wasn't easy for me. I'd lived my whole life thinking it was up to me.

That scripture became my anchor: *"Trust in the Lord with all your heart and lean not on your own understanding; in all your ways submit to Him, and He will make your paths straight."* – Proverbs 3:5-6

My role wasn't to have all the answers—it was to trust the One who does. And as I surrendered, God shifted things. He opened doors I couldn't have forced open. He brought clarity where confusion once reigned.

What looked like setbacks were setups for something greater. Maybe delayed by my own stubbornness—but never denied.

The truth is that most people never tap into the full potential of their lives and businesses because they don't understand the power of faith. They operate within their limits instead of stepping into God's limitless possibilities. Faith enables us to embrace the unknown, to take risks, to believe we were created for more than just "getting by."

Jesus said it best:

"Truly I tell you, if you have faith as small as a mustard seed, you can say to this mountain, 'Move from here to there,' and it will move. Nothing will be impossible for you." – Matthew 17:20

Faith moves mountains. Not just spiritually—but practically, in daily life and business. It gives us resilience, wisdom, and peace when the future is uncertain.

Ask yourself:

- Are you truly trusting in God's plan for your life and business? And how do you track and grow from these experiences?

- Do you make decisions based on faith, or does fear and doubt hold you back? How do you track and apply these learnings?

- Are you willing to embrace the refining process, knowing that every challenge is an opportunity for growth? How will you track any apply this valuable data?

When faith becomes the cornerstone of your life and business, everything shifts. Obstacles become stepping stones. Success is redefined—not as mere financial gain, but as alignment with God's purpose.

FAITH AS THE ULTIMATE VISIONARY TOOL – SEEING BEYOND THE PRESENT

One of the greatest gifts that faith offers is the ability to see beyond what is directly in front of us. Visionaries, leaders, and entrepreneurs all share a common trait: the ability to look beyond the present moment and believe in a future that has not yet been realized. This kind of foresight is not born from logic alone; it is the result of unwavering faith.

The Bible tells us in Hebrews 11:1, *"Now faith is the substance of things hoped for, the evidence of things not seen."* This means that faith is not just an idea—but also an action, it is an active force that gives substance to our hopes and visions. It allows us to trust that God is already working things out for our good, even when we cannot yet see the outcome.

Faith enables us to dream bigger, to step out boldly, and to build with confidence. It separates those who wait for ideal conditions from those who act in faith, knowing that God provides as we move forward. The ability to see beyond the present is what allows us to walk in obedience, trusting that God's plan is always greater than our own.

My greatest calling began ten years ago, when God spoke to me more clearly and powerfully than ever before. In that moment, I knew—everything in my life up to that point had been leading to this. This experience. This calling. This divine voice reaching out to me— me, someone who felt completely unworthy—opened the door to a reality I had never known, one I wasn't prepared for but couldn't ignore.

God was asking me to share everything I had learned—from business to life, from success to struggle—and give it freely to the world. It was more than I ever anticipated. It stretched me, demanded a level of faith I didn't know I had, and ushered me into something that felt so much bigger than myself. It felt next level—a calling far beyond my own strength or qualifications.

What I've come to understand is this: the real power isn't in showing up because I have it all together. It's in showing up faithfully because of who is within me. That might sound simple, but for most of my life, I carried the weight as if everything depended on me. I see now—it didn't have to be that hard. The cost didn't have to be so high.

I was operating from the wrong position, from a mindset that limited me. It wasn't my highest place of performance, purpose, or impact. But now, I understand. And from this place—of surrender, clarity, and calling—I lead differently.

God encourages us to trust Him with our visions and dreams. Luke 11:9 reminds us: *"So, I say to you: Ask and it will be given to you; seek and you will find; knock and the door will be opened to you."*

When we embrace our faith as our guiding force, we unlock the ability to see not just what is, but what could be. We begin to understand that our purpose extends beyond ourselves and that the work we do has a greater impact than we can see in the present.

This verse reinforces that faith is an active pursuit. We are not called to simply wish for things to happen; we are called to seek, to ask, and to move in faith. Faith requires action, and when we take those steps, God meets us there.

Ask yourself and document:

- How are you allowing temporary challenges to cloud your vision, or are you trusting that God is working behind the scenes?

- How are you stepping boldly into the unknown, or are you waiting for perfect conditions that may never come?

- Write down and document how you believe that your business, career, and life are part of a greater divine plan.

- Studies prove what gets measured, gets improved, how are you measuring and documenting your progress?

- Knowing, believing, and understanding Ephesians 3:20 *"Now to Him who is able to do exceedingly abundantly above all that we ask or think, according to the power that works in us,"* How will you proceed with that valuable truth moving forward?

Faith is the ultimate visionary tool. It allows us to dream bigger, to serve with greater intention, and to build something that extends beyond ourselves.

Now, let's explore the power of trusting the process—how faith in ourselves, others, and God's timing transforms the way we move forward.

Trusting the Process – Faith in Yourself, Others, and God's Timing

Trust is a fundamental component of faith. It requires us to let go of our desire for control and surrender to the process that God has set before us. Whether in life or business, we often find ourselves in seasons of waiting—times when things don't move as quickly as we would like or when doors seem to close without explanation. It is in these moments that faith teaches us to trust.

We must trust in three key areas: in ourselves, in others, and most importantly, in God's perfect timing. Each of these requires a level of surrender that is often uncomfortable but necessary for growth.

I've seen this truth play out countless times in my own journey. There were times when I wanted answers immediately when I felt frustrated that things weren't moving fast enough.

There was this time our construction team had worked so hard and spent a great deal of money preparing a proposal for a very nice size demolition and temporary office space project in a major department store. We thought for sure we were going to get the contract, but we didn't. Heart breaking.

It was a pivotal point in our business. Our Team was so disappointed and set back. It could have gone either way. But to this day I believe God had favor on people in our team and used that favor and blessing to change the direction, understanding and blessings in the lives of many of the people involved in that project.

We didn't receive that initial $40,000 contract—because they had something much bigger in mind. They wanted to bring us on for the full department store remodel. What would have started as a $40K job turned into a $578,000 first contract, followed by many more over the next 20+ years.

Looking back, I can clearly see how every delay, every redirection, and even every seeming setback was part of a greater plan. God was aligning things for something far beyond what I could have imagined at the time—His purpose unfolding step by step, even when I couldn't yet see it.

Proverbs 3:5-6 reminds us: *"Trust in the Lord with all your heart and lean not on your own understanding; in all your ways submit to him, and he will make your paths straight."*

This is a powerful truth. When we trust the process, we acknowledge that God's ways are beyond our comprehension. He sees the bigger picture. He knows what we need, when we need it, and how best to equip us for the road ahead.

But trusting the process also means having faith in ourselves and in others. It means believing that God has already given us the wisdom, talents, and abilities necessary to walk the path He has laid out for us. It means recognizing that He often works through people—mentors, business partners, employees, family members— who are placed in our lives for a reason.

In business, I have learned that trusting others is just as important as trusting God. Leaders who operate from a place of faith recognize that they cannot do everything alone. They build teams, delegate responsibilities, and trust that God has brought the right people into their lives for a purpose. They understand that success is not just about individual effort but about collective growth.

If we are constantly striving to control every aspect of our journey, we limit what God can do in our lives. But when we surrender, when we truly trust the process, we begin to see the beauty in divine timing. We stop forcing things to happen and start allowing God to unfold His plan in His way.

Isaiah 8:10 assures us: *"Devise your strategy, but it will be thwarted; propose your plan, but it will not stand, for God is with us."*

Ask yourself:

- Are you holding on too tightly to your own plans, or are you trusting in God's greater vision?

- Are you willing to wait, even when the waiting is difficult?

- Do you trust that God is using every challenge, every delay, and every detour for your ultimate good?

Faith in God's timing is one of the most powerful lessons we can learn. When we embrace it, we stop striving in our own strength and start walking in His. And that is where true peace and success are found.

Now, let's discuss what happens when challenges arise and how faith becomes our anchor in the storm.

When Challenges Arise – Faith as the Anchor in the Storm

No journey is without obstacles. In business and in life, we will inevitably encounter setbacks, failures, and hardships. It is in these moments—when everything seems uncertain or overwhelming—that faith becomes our anchor, keeping us grounded and steadfast. Faith does not eliminate challenges, but it equips us with the strength to endure them.

I have faced seasons of trials that tested every part of me—loss, financial hardships, business struggles, and personal tragedies. At times, the weight of these experiences made it feel impossible to move forward. But in those darkest moments, I found that faith wasn't just a concept—it was a source of strength, a foundation that kept me from breaking under pressure.

One of the most defining moments of my life was losing my father at a young age. I remember standing in the church, looking at his coffin, feeling the deepest sense of loss and uncertainty. How would life continue? How would we survive? Who will protect and take care of us. My mom brother and sister and myself? Will we be out on the streets? Big fears for a young child, losing your father.

As I lifted my eyes to the massive cross hanging at the front of the church—towering 30 feet high, with a man nailed to it—I thought to myself, *Yes, that's Jesus. The Son of God, sent to die for my sins. The one my parents and grandparents always told me about—my truth, my light, my comfort, my protector.*

And then, something remarkable happened.

A deep, unexplainable peace washed over me. I couldn't fully understand it in that moment, but now I know—it was God's presence. Quietly, powerfully, He was letting me know I wasn't alone.

Faith is what allows us to withstand the storms of life and

business. John 3:16 reminds us of the ultimate act of love and sacrifice: *"For God so loved the world that he gave his one and only Son, that whoever believes in him shall not perish but have eternal life."* If God would give us His Son to save us, how much more will He sustain us in our times of difficulty?

Difficulties in business can be just as testing. There were times when I faced financial struggles, uncertain markets, and tough leadership decisions. In those moments, I had a choice: to be paralyzed by fear or to trust that God was working behind the scenes. Every challenge became an opportunity to lean on faith rather than my own strength. And time and time again, God showed up—through unexpected provisions, open doors, and moments of clarity that I could not have orchestrated on my own.

Proverbs 3:5-6 instructs us: *"Trust in the Lord with all your heart and lean not on your own understanding; in all your ways submit to him, and he will make your paths straight."* When challenges arise, our natural instinct is to try to fix things on our own. But faith teaches us to trust in a higher plan, even when we can't see the full picture.

Ask yourself:

- How do you respond when faced with adversity—do you lean on faith or fall into fear?

- How are you allowing hardships to strengthen your trust in

God, or are they weakening your resolve?

- Can you look back on past trials and see how God was shaping and refining you through them?

Faith is not just about believing when things are going well. It is about holding on even when everything feels like it's falling apart. It is about knowing that God is working through every trial and that the storm will pass. With faith, we don't just survive challenges—we emerge stronger, wiser, and more aligned with God's plan.

Now, let's explore how faith and integrity work hand in hand in aligning our gifts with God's perfect plan.

FAITH AND INTEGRITY – ALIGNING YOUR GIFTS WITH GOD'S PERFECT PLAN

Faith and integrity go hand in hand. When we align our lives and businesses with God's will, we operate from a place of honesty, excellence, and purpose. Integrity is more than just doing the right thing when others are watching—it is about living in a way that reflects our faith in every decision we make.

God has given each of us unique gifts and talents. He has placed within us the ability to create, lead, and impact others. But how we use these gifts matters. Are we using them for self-gain, or are we stewarding them in a way that glorifies God and serves others?

James 4:2 reminds us: *"You do not have because you do not ask God."* Many people struggle with their purpose because they are not seeking God's guidance. They rely solely on their own understanding, trying to control outcomes rather than trusting that God has already equipped them with everything they need.

I have seen businesses built on greed, dishonesty, and short-term thinking. While some of them may achieve temporary success, they lack sustainability. Without integrity, businesses crumble under the weight of unethical decisions. But I have also seen businesses that prioritize faith, integrity, and service thrive in ways that extend beyond financial success. These businesses leave a lasting impact because they are aligned with God's perfect plan.

Faith-driven integrity means making decisions based on principles rather than profit. It means treating employees, clients, and partners with respect and honesty. It means trusting that when we do things the right way, God will provide. Isaiah 8:10 reassures us: *"Devise your strategy, but it will be thwarted; propose your plan, but it will not stand, for God is with us."* When we operate outside of God's will, our efforts are in vain. But when we align with His purpose, success follows in ways we never imagined.

I remember a time when I was faced with a difficult business decision. I had the opportunity to take a shortcut that could have led to quick financial gain, but it didn't sit right with me.

We had been working with a client for a couple of years when he switched companies. At his new role, he began giving us construction projects through his new employer. The complication? He still owed my company around $72,000 in change order work from a project we had completed for his previous employer.

Then something strange happened—we received a contract from his new company for work we had never actually done. Technically, we could have billed against it and recovered more than what was owed from the previous project.

I paused. I prayed. I sought wisdom.

And in the end, I chose to walk away.

At first, it felt like a financial loss. But looking back now, I see it for what it truly was—a test of integrity. And God honored that decision. He opened doors I never could have imagined and led me into opportunities that far outweighed what I gave up.

Integrity isn't always the most convenient path. But it's the one that leads to lasting success—the kind money can't buy.

Ask yourself and write it down or document:

- Are your business and personal decisions aligned with your faith? Where might you struggle and why?

- Do you trust that God will bless integrity, even if it requires sacrifice? Think about it and write it down, where has he, and where hasn't he and why do you think?

- Do you know what your spiritual gifts and talents are? Identify where and how you and using your gifts and talents in a way that serves others and honors God?

- What areas would you like expand your knowledge growth with the Lord

- What types of resources would you like to receive and why?

Faith calls us to live and lead with integrity. When we align our gifts, talents, and actions with God's perfect plan, we find success that is deeper than financial gain—it is the fulfillment of our true purpose. Now, let's take a deeper look at how faith applies to our daily growth and walk with God.

WALKING IN DIVINE PURPOSE – APPLYING FAITH TO DAILY GROWTH

Faith is not just a belief—it is a daily practice, a way of living that requires intention and commitment. Walking in divine purpose means aligning our everyday actions with our faith, allowing God to guide our decisions, and seeking His presence in every aspect of our lives and businesses.

A life of faith is not passive; it demands action. Luke 11:9 reminds us: *"So I say to you: Ask and it will be given to you; seek and you will find; knock and the door will be opened to you."* This scripture calls us to be active participants in our faith. We must seek God, ask for wisdom, and step forward in obedience, trusting that He will open the right doors at the right time.

Applying faith to daily growth means cultivating habits that draw us closer to God. Consistent in duration, times, schedule creating habits help, and include:

Starting each day with prayer and gratitude, acknowledging that every opportunity and challenge is part of God's plan.

Making decisions through the lens of faith, trusting that God's wisdom surpasses our own.

Seeking God's Word for guidance, allowing scripture to shape our thoughts, attitudes, and choices.

Practicing patience and perseverance, understanding that growth takes time and that God's timing is perfect.

Serving others with love and integrity, using our gifts to uplift those around us.

For me, reading the Word of God—the Bible—is the most direct and powerful way to connect with His truth. While there are many valuable resources out there—books, sermons, audio teachings, and videos that support and deepen our understanding—nothing should distract us from the pure truth of God's Word. As it says in John 4:14, *"when we seek Him, He satisfies a thirst in us that nothing else can."*

My walk with God has been a journey. And through it all, He has always been there. The real challenge has never been His presence— it's been about my priorities. Where does God sit in my life? Is He first? Somewhere in the middle? Or, if I'm honest, sometimes last?

That's where free will comes in. God rarely forces His way in. He waits—lovingly, patiently—for us to choose Him. And the choice is always ours. He asks us to seek Him first. But knowing that isn't enough. We must act. We must pick up our cross and follow Him daily.

What I've come to realize is this: it's actually easier than we think. Because we're not walking in our own strength—we walk in His. We're not qualified by our own merit—we're qualified by the sacrifice Jesus made at the cross. And that truth changes everything.

Faith in daily growth also means embracing challenges as opportunities to trust God more deeply. There will be moments when things don't go as planned, when business setbacks occur, or when personal struggles test our endurance. But it is in these moments that our faith is strengthened. Proverbs 3:5-6 teaches us: *"Trust in the Lord with all your heart and lean not on your own understanding; in all your ways submit to him, and he will make your paths straight."* When we surrender our plans to God, He leads us in the right direction, even when we can't see the full path ahead.

I've learned that growth doesn't always come from success—it often comes from the trials that push us beyond our comfort zones. I've experienced seasons where I questioned whether I was on the right path, but by remaining faithful and continuing to seek God, I found clarity and strength that could only come from Him.

Ask yourself and would suggest writing them down:

- Are you inviting God into your daily decisions? When and how?

- Are you actively seeking growth in your faith? How are you doing that, and how has it helped you in your journey?

- Or are you staying stagnant? Please identify how that is impacting your life and perhaps what you need to do next, and by when?

- Are you willing to trust God's process, even when it doesn't align with your timeline? How will you do that?

- Do you have the resources you need to do so. Do you know where to get the resources needed? How can we help?

Walking in divine purpose requires us to take daily steps of faith, trusting that God is leading us toward something greater. When we commit to living out our faith in both our personal and professional lives, we experience transformation that goes beyond success—it leads to a life of fulfillment, impact, and deep spiritual growth.

Now, let's explore how we can leave a legacy of faith that extends beyond our own lives and into the lives of future generations.

Leaving a Legacy of Faith – Building Beyond Yourself

At the end of our journey, what truly matters is not how much we have accumulated but the impact we have made. A life and business built on faith leave a legacy that extends beyond personal success. When we lead with faith, our influence reaches far beyond our own lifetime, shaping generations to come.

Faith-driven individuals understand that their work is about more than just themselves. They mentor, they give back, and they lift others up. They create businesses that serve communities, empower people, and reflect God's love. This kind of leadership does not happen by chance—it is intentional and rooted in a commitment to honoring God in all we do.

Leaving a legacy of faith means living in a way that inspires others to seek God. It means demonstrating integrity, perseverance, and love in all that we do. It means being a mentor, a leader, and a servant. It means recognizing that success is not just about personal achievements but about the lives we touch along the way.

I've had the privilege of witnessing the power of faith-driven leadership up close. The most impactful leaders I've known weren't defined by wealth or influence, but by how they invested in others. They led with humility, served with integrity, and understood that their purpose reached far beyond personal gain. Their leadership left a lasting legacy—one built on character, not status.

Legacy often gets overlooked—not because it doesn't matter, but because many people simply don't know what a meaningful legacy looks like. That's why we turn to Scripture, which offers powerful guidance on the kind of legacy that truly endures.

Ecclesiastes reminds us that wisdom is far more valuable than wealth. In chapter 7, it says: *"Wisdom, like an inheritance, is a good thing ... Wisdom is a shelter as money is a shelter, but the advantage of knowledge is this: wisdom preserves those who have it"* (Ecclesiastes 7:11–12). Similarly, Proverbs teaches that wisdom is *"more precious than rubies"* (3:15), and that it *"walks in the way of righteousness … bestowing a rich inheritance on those who love me"* (Proverbs 8:20–21). True wealth, according to Scripture, is found in wisdom, justice, and reverence for the Lord.

Proverbs 14:26 reinforces this truth: *"Whoever fears the Lord has a secure fortress, and for their children it will be a refuge." And* the psalmist Asaph emphasizes the importance of generational legacy—not of possessions, but of passing down the knowledge of God's power and His laws (Psalm 78:4–6).

These verses show us that the most enduring legacy we can leave is not material—it's spiritual. Wisdom, righteousness, and the fear of the Lord outlast any inheritance we could store in a bank account.

Ask yourself and write it down:

- What kind of legacy are you building?

- How are you doing that?

- What elements will you add to empower your desired life legacy?

- Are you using your faith to uplift and mentor others, and if so, identify how?

- Will the impact of your life extend beyond your time on earth? if so, how?

A legacy of faith is not about wealth or status; it is about influence and impact. It is about planting seeds that will grow long after we are gone. When we live by faith, we create a ripple effect—one that can transform families, businesses, and entire communities.

Now, let's reflect on the key lessons from this chapter and how we can apply them to our lives moving forward.

WALKING FORWARD IN FAITH

As we reflect on the journey of faith in life and business, one truth remains constant: faith is the foundation that sustains us, the vision that guides us, the trust that strengthens us, and the legacy that outlives us. Faith is not passive; it is an active force that shapes how we live, lead, and make decisions. It is the difference between a life of uncertainty and one rooted in divine purpose.

Through this chapter, we have explored the power of faith in decision-making. We have seen how faith provides the strength to endure challenges, the courage to see beyond the present, and the wisdom to trust God's timing. We have recognized the importance of integrity, the necessity of daily spiritual growth, and the impact of leaving a legacy that extends beyond ourselves.

My faith has been profoundly shaped not only by my successes and challenges in business but also by deeply personal experiences—especially the separation from my kids and the time shared with my mother before her passing. The loss of my dad. These were some of the most painful and defining moments of my life. The void created by separation and loss could have led to despair, but instead, it became an opportunity for my faith to deepen. Through the pain, loss and uncertainty. I learned what it means to fully surrender to God's will, to trust Him even when I did not understand, and to find peace in His presence despite the circumstances.

Proverbs 3:5-6 reminds us: *"Trust in the Lord with all your heart and lean not on your own understanding; in all your ways submit to him, and he will make your paths straight."* This scripture calls us to surrender, to trust in God's plan, and to walk forward in faith—even when we cannot see the full picture.

If there is one thing I want you to take away from this chapter, it is this: faith is not just about believing in God—it is about walking with Him. It is about seeking Him daily, making decisions through His wisdom, and trusting that He is always working for our good. Not being qualified or earned, but by God's grace, love, and tender mercy, and HEIS sons' sacrifice at the cross.

Ask yourself and write it down:

- Are you allowing faith to guide your decisions, or are you relying solely on your own understanding?

- How can you improve that? And will you?

- Are you stepping out in faith, even when the path is unclear?

- Identify how that has helped you?

- Are you committed to living a life and building a business that reflects your faith and please share how, moving forward?

Faith does not promise an easy path, but it guarantees that we never walk alone. As you move forward, let faith be the foundation of your life, the guiding force behind your decisions, and the legacy you leave behind. When we choose faith, we choose purpose, impact, and a life aligned with God's perfect plan.

To God go the glory for all that HE is, has done, is doing, and will continue to do in our lives. Keep your faith as a verb—alive, active, and unwavering.

ABOUT MARK MAES

Mark Maes is a builder—not just of businesses, but of people, purpose, and legacy. As the Founder and CEO of Maes and Associates, Mark leads one of the top consulting and management firms known for helping CEOs, executives, and teams turn big visions into results that matter. With over 40 years of hands-on leadership experience, he's the go-to strategist for those ready to lead with clarity, integrity, and impact.

Before launching Maes and Associates in 2009, Mark spent more than three decades at the helm of M&M Interiors—a company he built from the ground up into the fourth-largest non-union C-9 contractor in California. His leadership wasn't just strategic—it was transformational. Fueled by faith and grounded in values, Mark created an environment where excellence, accountability, and vision weren't just talked about—they were lived.

Today, Mark applies that same approach through his groundbreaking system, High Five Priority Business Mapping™—a framework that helps leaders define What Perfect Looks Like (WPLL), align their goals, and implement actionable steps that drive real, measurable results. From boardrooms to construction sites, his system has reshaped the way leaders think, plan, and lead.

He's also the creator of H5 LMS, an on-demand learning platform that equips leaders at all levels with the practical tools they need to lead well—without the fluff. Whether you're a startup founder or a seasoned executive, Mark's teachings meet you where you are and move you forward with precision and purpose.

A contributing author of the Amazon #1 bestseller The New C-Suite: Civil Leadership in Action, Mark's influence extends far beyond business. His years in elite leadership circles like T.E.C. and Biblically Based Leadership (BBL) have deepened his belief that faith and business aren't separate—they're stronger together.

Mark lives his life and leads his company by one guiding truth: To God be the glory. His mission is simple but powerful—help people lead with purpose, build with vision, and live with legacy.

Faithful Ambition

By Tiana Sanchez

What does ambition mean to you? When you hear that word, do you immediately think of someone who is goal-oriented and determined? Do you picture a person with big dreams—someone eager to rise in their career and transform their circumstances?

Ambition comes in many forms, and in this chapter, I want to unpack four distinct types: good ambition, reckless ambition, circumstantial ambition, and faithful ambition.

Good ambition is powered by a personal drive to achieve something meaningful however not all ambition is good ambition. **Reckless ambition**, on the other hand, is fueled by an unhealthy need to outshine others. **Circumstantial ambition** arises out of a sense of duty or obligation to someone or something.

We should strive for a personal drive to achieve something that is not fueled by competition or necessity—that's **faithful ambition**. Faithful ambition is the pursuit of something great without compromising what truly matters most. Reckless ambition and circumstantial ambition are easily misaligned with your core values, often leading to burnout, resentment, or regret—because they're driven by ego or external pressure rather than purpose. Faithful ambition, on the other hand, is rooted in clarity, conviction, and a higher calling—making it the type of ambition we should strive for.

Faithful ambition means striving for success while staying true to core values. It requires discernment, resilience, and the courage to stand firm when challenges arise. I remember when I started my business in 2011 after being laid off from the financial industry. With no business experience or degree, I pursued entrepreneurship. I secured my business license, gained my first client, and eventually expanded, serving over 100 clients and impacting more than 10,000 employees.

At times, I faced difficult decisions. Some contracts did not align with my value, and I made the difficult choice to decline them. Other contracts jeopardized the integrity of my work, forcing me to make hard choices.

One example involved a local government agency navigating the aftermath of an officer-involved shooting within the community they served. My firm was hired to facilitate focus groups, conduct assessments, and support the organization. The project faced delays beyond our control, and some members of my team were treated poorly.

Weeks of tension built to a breaking point, and I considered withdrawing from the contract despite being three-fourths complete. The stress was overwhelming. Instead of withdrawing from the contact, I requested a month-long pause to regroup and re-strategize. I had the discernment that my team was burnt out and the courage to take a break. That decision allowed us to return and complete the work without sacrificing integrity or the reputation my firm had upheld for over a decade. We remained vigilant and focused on the outcome.

Faithful ambition is a pursuit, **not a compromise** — where one surrenders to external expectations. In essence, faithful ambition is the **pursuit** of meaningful goals without conforming to others' definitions of success. Let's explore the word 'pursue' for a moment. Did you know that the word **pursue** is mentioned 143 times in the Bible? It means to chase or press forward. Have you ever pursued something with all of your might? Think of the last time you lost your car keys or your cell phone. Remember how you tore through the house—checking under sofas, rifling through cabinets, and looking in places you knew, deep down, they probably weren't? That relentless determination, that sense of urgency—you were completely focused on finding what mattered in that moment.

In the natural and in a worldly view, some see ambition as excessive, yet with God, all things are possible. He expects us to live abundantly, excel in all things, and receive the desires of our hearts. Why would God exceed expectations, granting us more than we ask, think, or imagine if He didn't want us to be ambitious? The obstacles arise when your ambition confuses others. It can cause conflict when personal aspirations disrupt others' plans for you. It may trigger envy, resentment, or serve as a barrier when peers expect conformity to their standards of achievement.

In my experience, I have learned that ambition is not binary or one-dimensional. It has complexities much like we do. Let's explore the different types of ambition and examples:

Good Ambition - A pursuit predicated on your personal desires, propelled by your goals, and often accompanied by the possibility of compromise along the way. For example: You start a wellness brand because you've always wanted to help people live healthier lives. You're willing to work long hours, take calculated risks, and even pivot your product line to meet market demands, as long as it keeps you moving forward.

Reckless Ambition – Competitive in an unhealthy way, rooted in envy. It thrives on surpassing others, focusing on personal gain at any cost. For example: You launch a tech startup with the sole purpose of outdoing a rival company. You cut corners, overpromise to investors, and push your team past burnout—all to prove you're better, regardless of the consequences.

Circumstantial Ambition – Driven by obligation. The need to earn more, secure promotions, or provide for others overrides personal aspirations. Imagine, you started a side business not out of passion, but because your family needs more income. You're not particularly invested in the work, but you feel compelled to keep it going for financial stability and social expectation.

Faithful Ambition - Faithful ambition is a long-term pursuit of something great—driven by conviction, grounded in faith, and unwavering in its refusal to conform to others' expectations or compromise what truly matters. Let's say, you build a social enterprise that creates jobs for formerly incarcerated individuals. Despite slower growth and external pressure to scale faster or focus solely on profit, you remain committed to your mission and your values

Understanding the different types of ambition will give you clarity and help evaluate where you are and where you want to be.

Looking back, choosing faithful ambition in that situation with the client, that everything would work out, and refusing to compromise, was the right course to take. But it's not always easy to know the right course. It helps to have a compass, a guide that directs your path. Thankfully, God has given us all we need. In the next few sections, we'll talk about Faith as a Compass, the Power of Discernment, Building a Strong 'Hero' Support System, and having Success on Your Own Terms.

FAITH AS A COMPASS

A compass acts as a guide, pointing you in the right direction even when the path ahead is unclear—helping you stay on course. Have you ever been so lost and fearful because you didn't know where you were going yet you trusted in God to bring you through?

When I was seven, my mother decided to take us to the LA County Zoo. It was me, my older sister, and my younger brother. We were excited about the trip, and it was the first time my mother drove us there. We explored the zoo, played, and enjoyed a picnic before it was time to leave. As the sun set, we packed up and headed home. As we got in the car to leave, my mom got turned around. She had taken the streets to get to the zoo but couldn't retrace her route—meaning we'd have to take the freeway. The problem was that my mom was terrified of the freeway.

Realizing her predicament as darkness approached, she pulled over at a payphone—yes, back when payphones were still common—to call my uncle for directions. When she returned to the car, she realized that in fact she would have to take the freeway home and panic set in.

I remember her gripping the steering wheel at 10 and 2, adjusting the mirrors, sitting up straight, and shushing us kids in the backseat—even though I don't recall us making noise. She was terrified and honestly, so were we. Through silence and prayer, we finally made it home. It was a miracle! My mother was likely more relieved than she let on, but that day, I made a vow. At nearly 49 years old, I have kept it: I have never driven to the zoo with my mother again.

Back then, there was no navigation, Siri or Google maps. We used our memory, landmarks, and written directions to get around. What my mother needed was a compass — something guiding her every turn. The only compass she had available at that time was her faith - her belief that she would make it home safely. The lesson is that faith coupled with ambition creates direction with purpose—a steady pursuit guided by conviction, not just desire. I've learned that when fear tries to take the wheel, **faith does not fail** — it gives us direction.

Faith Doesn't Fail

Faith provides the guidance we need to reach our destination, much like a compass in both life and business. One of my favorite scriptures that best describes faith is found in Hebrews 11:1, *"Faith is the substance of things hoped for, the evidence of things not seen."* You will be faced with situations that often leave you feeling lost, unsure of where you are or where you're headed. You need a guide, a compass to help you navigate. Faith serves as that compass and that compass never fails!

Before heading somewhere unfamiliar, we wouldn't just drive aimlessly—we'd check directions, use a GPS, and follow a plan. A lesson I learned the hard way when I took my first driving test at age 16. Looking back, I felt prepared, even overprepared, since my friends had shared all the driving routes and parking tricks. The test went smoothly for the first 15 minutes until I missed a second red light right after a no-turn-on-red sign. As soon as I ran it, I knew I had failed. I nervously asked the instructor, *"Did I fail?"* He stayed silent, jotting notes. When we arrived back at the DMV, I asked again. This time, he confirmed it. My heart sank.

But faith doesn't work that way. FAITH DOESN'T FAIL. It's not about passing or failing a test. It's about believing in what's unseen, trusting in what's ahead. Again, *"faith is the substance of things hoped for, the evidence of things not seen."* If we had to pass a test every time we drove, constantly fearing failure, we'd never move forward. Many of us approach faith this way—understanding its fundamentals but not applying it daily. Faith is an action, and actions must be applied to something. One thing I've come to realize is that faith often lacks a clear application—something we're about to explore next.

The Missing Application

Many people are **aware of faith**, but far fewer apply it. They know the verses, recite the prayers, and attend church, yet when life throws them off course, they scramble for direction like someone lost without GPS. They believe in faith conceptually but hesitate when it's time to live it out. They are familiar with the fundamentals, but when the road ahead is unclear, they hesitate. They grip the wheel in fear, trying to control everything instead of surrendering to God's direction. They treat faith like an optional tool rather than the very thing designed to guide them.

Knowing how to drive doesn't mean you'll never get lost. My mother knew how to operate a car, but she avoided the freeway at all costs. When she had no choice but to face it, panic set in. Had she studied a map daily, familiarizing herself with different routes in advance before getting lost, she might have been more confident, less afraid, and better prepared to navigate the unfamiliar road ahead.

The goal is to apply faith daily. That looks like:

Start your morning with intention – Spend a few quiet minutes in prayer, reflection, or journaling. Set a daily affirmation rooted in faith, such as *"I trust that everything is working for my good."*

Take one faith-driven action each day – Make a phone call, send an email, invest time in a project, or say yes to an opportunity—even if it feels uncomfortable. Faith grows when it's practiced.

Prepare for what you're praying for – Study, train, research, or organize. Show up as if the opportunity is already on its way.

Speak life into your day – Replace negative self-talk with words that align with faith: *"I am capable," "I'm on the right path," "Even this has a purpose."*

Practice gratitude at night – Before bed, write down three things you're thankful for—even if the day was hard. Gratitude keeps faith alive, especially when things don't go as planned.

Surround yourself with faith-filled voices – Listen to podcasts, read books, or talk with people who challenge and encourage your belief, not your fear.

It's not enough to understand faith—you have to apply it. It's not just about quoting scriptures or believing in theory. It's about moving forward, even when you can't see the outcome. When I failed my driving test, I immediately knew why. I had all the knowledge, but I didn't apply the knowledge accurately. We have access to faith, yet we often fail to apply it because we are too focused on our own fears and uncertainties.

Faith doesn't work like a test you can fail. Faith isn't about proving yourself—it's about trusting God.

So, the questions are: Are you just aware of faith, or are you applying it? Are you checking the map daily, or are you waiting until you feel lost? The real measure of faith isn't in the knowing—it's in the doing. And it's the doing that reassures and reaffirms our faith.

The Reassurance of Faith

Fear is rooted in uncertainty and doubt, while the assurance of faith is grounded in trust in God. Fear questions what might go wrong while faith believes in what will go right—even when the outcome isn't yet visible. Faith is believing in what's unseen and that's difficult to do. I can recall a time that I didn't act in faith but in fear. I was traveling to Las Vegas for a business trip by myself. This trip pushed me outside my comfort zone because I flew there on a buddy pass, meaning I wasn't guaranteed a seat on the plane.

Before I get into the story, there's something you need to know about me. I have a fear of flying. I loathe it. I avoid flying at all costs. When I fly, I start preparing days—sometimes even weeks—in advance. First, I mentally prepare by praying over the flight and reciting affirmations to calm my nerves. Second, I avoid eating 24 hours beforehand and barely speak on the day of travel. Lastly, I listen to my gospel playlist from the time I arrive at the airport until the plane lands safely at our destination.

Now that we have that out of the way, back to the trip.

Remarkably, I made it to Las Vegas to attend the conference using the buddy pass. After the conference, I headed back to the airport and waited anxiously for my name to be called but it wasn't. So, I waited for the next flight, but my name wasn't called again, and I missed that flight, too. Frustrated and desperate, I went against what I knew was right—to wait, be patient, and trust that all things would work out for my good. Instead, I rented a car and drove home alone. That decision was a mistake, driven not by faith, but by fear. What should have been a one-hour flight turned into a five-hour drive through rain, sleet, and even snow. This experience reinforced a powerful lesson: **when we try to speed up faith instead of resting in the assurance of faith, we get delays, unnecessary detours, and disappointment.**

To avoid the delays, unnecessary detours, and disappointment that come from acting out of fear instead of faith, I want to share a simple mantra that helped me as a kid who struggled with directions.

"Never Eat Shredded Wheat."

It's a phrase I learned to remember North, East, South, and West (NESW). That little saying became my anchor. Because if I could identify just one direction, I could figure out the rest. And that's the reassurance of faith—when you're grounded in one truth, it helps you navigate everything else.

Here's a way to remember incorporating your faith in everything you do:

N – Navigate life with trust, not fear.

E – Embrace challenges as part of the journey.

S – Stand firm in belief, even when the path is unclear.

W – Walk forward with courage, knowing faith leads the way.

Faith doesn't always eliminate fear, but it gives us something stronger to stand on when fear shows up. But faith alone isn't always enough—we also need discernment. Because sometimes, the choice isn't between right and wrong, but between good and best. In the next section, we'll explore The Power of Discernment—the ability to use wisdom when the options aren't always clear and the stakes feel high.

The Power of Discernment

Faithful ambition isn't just about pursuing something great—it's about pursuing it wisely. And that's where discernment comes in. While ambition drives us forward, discernment helps us know when to pause, when to proceed, and who we can trust along the way. When I was 16, I got a frantic call from my boyfriend. He told me he was going to kill himself after hearing a false rumor that I had been unfaithful. I was at home with a friend, and she could see the panic on my face. Without hesitation, I said, "I need to go see him!"

Like most teenagers, I pushed boundaries. I had an older sister, and sometimes I used her ID to get into 18-and-over clubs. My father always insisted I couldn't have a boyfriend until I turned 16. But by then, he was absent, and I lacked the protection and guidance young girls crave. Against my better judgment, I convinced my friend to drive me to the club where I found my boyfriend—drunk, unstable, and inconsolable. I reassured him that the rumor wasn't true, but he wouldn't listen. Somehow, I managed to calm him down, avoiding another crisis.

That wasn't the only time. Throughout our four-year relationship, I felt like a character trapped in a psychological thriller. I had no idea that young teenage men can be possessive and insecure. I remember prom night vividly. Before heading to an after-party, we stopped at a friend's house for a quick outfit check and to get our plans together for the rest of the night. Sometime during our brief stay at my friend's house, we got into an argument and we never made it to the after-party. Instead, I found myself as a passenger in a car, with my boyfriend speeding down the road and running red lights. I thought, this is it. I'm going to die. Nothing I said or did would stop him. I prepared for the worst. I'm going to die. Looking back, I know my mother's prayers kept me safe that night.

After the relationship ended right after high school, he stalked me. He left threatening messages, used intimidation, and harassed members of my family. It was unhealthy, but relationships like that don't appear out of nowhere—there are always warning signs. I ignored them. In hindsight, the signs pointed to underlying mental illness, later confirmed by his family's medical history. Years after we lost touch, I learned that his marriage ended in tragedy—his life cut short. I often reflect on what I missed. Was I blinded by love? Did I ignore the signs, hoping he would change?

Discernment is the ability to distinguish between right and wrong, good and evil. *"Teach me knowledge and good judgment, for I trust your commands."* – Psalms 119:66. *"Dear friends, do not believe every spirit, but test the spirits to see whether they are from God, because many false prophets have gone out into the world."* – 1 John 4:1. Both scriptures give us examples of discernment—it's that inner voice, that nudge that something isn't right. It requires wisdom to evaluate situations from all angles and make sound decisions. When anchored in faith and values, the choice may not be easy, but it's clear. Discernment isn't just for extreme or dangerous situations— it's just as critical when the temptation is subtle and the stakes feel personal. I discovered this again in my late twenties, when an unexpected opportunity challenged not only my ambition, but my integrity when I was striving to build the life I had always dreamed of.

An Indecent Proposal

Faithful ambition requires more than just drive—it demands discernment. Because every opportunity isn't a divine assignment, and sometimes what looks like a blessing is really a test of character.

As a teenager, I had big dreams of becoming a choreographer or a child psychologist. Neither panned out. By my late 20s, I had no degree and wasn't living the life I wanted. I married young, divorced after three years, and became a single mom working in banking. Then, an opportunity presented itself. It was an indecent proposal.

When I worked in banking, assisting VIP clients was part of my job. Taking them to lunch or dinner built relationships that kept their business with the bank. One evening, I took a high-profile client to dinner. He was married with two kids. This wasn't unusual as this was regularly practiced as a way to discuss business in an informal setting. After about an hour, our conversation shifted from casual to personal. He asked about my future, and I admitted that I wasn't where I wanted to be. He offered to change that. He could take care of me, provide financial security—on one condition: we have a secret affair.

For a moment, I weighed how being a "kept woman" could improve my situation. As a single mom, the financial security was tempting. Could I live with myself if I entered a relationship with a married man? What would that even look like? It felt like a scene from Indecent Proposal—minus the million dollars. It was tempting, but I couldn't get over the fact that it was WRONG. I had to stand on principle and fight that desire.

Before you judge me and wonder how I could even consider such a thing, take a moment to reflect on how easily compromise can creep in when trying to improve a situation.

For you—or someone you know—it might look different: Maybe it's accepting a kickback or bribe to close a deal. Perhaps it's hiring an unqualified friend because you know they'll follow orders without question. Or maybe it's staying silent about a boss's unethical behavior to protect your promotion.

Temptation is inevitable. In Matthew 4:1-11 and Luke 4:1-13, Jesus was tempted by Satan, yet He always responded with, *"It is written…"*—reminding the tempter that he held no power.

Our principles shape our decisions. They serve as anchors, with faith as our compass. Some choices seem good on the surface, but are they really? How do we know if our ambitions align with what's right? Put them through a litmus test:

Alignment – Does this ambition align with God's purpose for my life?

Accountability – Do I have trusted people who will challenge me if I go off course?

Integrity – Am I making a meaningful sacrifice for the greater good, or am I compromising my values?

Direction – Will this pursuit lead me closer to my purpose or steer me down the wrong path?

Scripture reminds us to lean not on our own understanding. *"Trust in the LORD with all your heart and lean not on your own understanding; in all your ways submit to him, and he will make your paths straight."* – Proverbs 3:5-6. I often pray for discernment, and you can too. Here's a prayer for wisdom in decision-making:

Lord, grant me the wisdom to see beyond appearances and the courage to follow Your truth. When faced with choices, help me discern between compromise and conviction, between fleeting desires and lasting purpose. Surround me with trusted voices who will guide me when I stray. Let my ambitions align with Your will, and may my steps be anchored in faith, not fear. Teach me to test what is before me, knowing that not all that glitters is good. Strengthen my heart to reject what leads me astray and embrace what draws me closer to You. Amen.

Pursuing faithful ambition doesn't mean doing it all on your own. In fact, the greater the calling, the more essential it becomes to surround yourself with people who strengthen your faith, sharpen your focus, and walk with you through the highs and lows.

Building a Strong Support System

"Two are better than one, and a cord of three strands is not easily broken." – Ecclesiastes 4:12. This scripture reminds us of the power

of support systems. We aren't meant to navigate life alone—especially when pursuing big ambitions.

Think back to the last time you lay shivering under cold, heavy covers, desperately trying to get warm. How much warmer would you feel with someone beside you, acting as a shield, offering comfort and protection? A strong support system works the same way. It provides a covering when challenges arise and a safeguard against compromises that could steer you off course. Faith is our compass, but friends serve as the **hero support** that keeps us steady.

Hero Support vs. Sidekicks

When my oldest son was younger, one of his favorite movies was Sky High, a story about a teenager born to superhero parents who hadn't yet developed powers of his own. Expectations weighed heavily on him, but in time, he discovered his strength and eventually, the ability to fly.

The movie also introduced a different perspective on sidekicks. Instead of dismissing them as lesser characters, they were called **hero support**—individuals who played critical roles in a superhero's journey. I prefer this term because having someone's back is not a secondary role—it's essential.

In life, our hero support system consists of people who guide, challenge, and encourage us. They help us move forward in moments of doubt, hold us accountable, and ensure we don't lose sight of what matters. You can look at this as three essential roles which play the part of the Mechanic, the Instructor, and the Counselor.

THE MECHANIC: THE ONE WHO PREPARES AND REPAIRS

The mechanic in your support system plays a vital role at the beginning and end of your pursuits. Just like you take your car to a mechanic for a tune-up before a road trip, this person ensures you're equipped for the journey ahead. They check under the hood, inspect for weaknesses, and help prevent breakdowns before they happen. They are also the ones you turn to when something goes wrong— when you hit roadblocks, need repairs, or feel like quitting.

Biblical Example: Noah - Noah was handpicked by God to build the ark—a task that required vision, preparation, and endurance. He gathered materials, followed precise instructions, and ensured the ark was ready for what lay ahead. The mechanics in your life do the same. They equip you, challenge you, and ensure you don't set out unprepared.

Real-life example: Let's say you hire a mentor or coach before a big career move. The career coach helps you prepare by reviewing your resume, role-play tough conversations, and point out blind spots in your leadership style. You're a new leader and don't like dealing with difficult team members so they're the first person you call to help you get back on track.

THE INSTRUCTOR: THE ONE WHO GUIDES YOU FORWARD

The Instructor or Siri-type friends ride with you on the journey. They give direction, offer insight, and encourage movement. Like a GPS, they translate complex situations into clear next steps. They know you well enough to guide you in a way that makes sense and keeps you on track.

Faith acts as our internal compass, but Siri friends are the voice that verbalizes where to turn next. When you're uncertain, they provide clarity and patience, helping you take that next difficult step.

Biblical Example: The Holy Spirit - Scripture describes the Holy Spirit as our guide. Just as He leads us in truth, Siri friends help us navigate life's decisions with wisdom and perspective.

Real-life example: Imagine you're navigating a new project and feeling overwhelmed by the process, timeline and direction. A colleague, who's already done something similar, shares their process, offers practical steps, and checks in regularly to make sure you're staying on course. They don't just cheer you on, they give you advice, reassurance, and helps you take the next step when you feel like it's too difficult.

THE COUNSELOR: THE ONE WHO OFFERS WISDOM

The counselor helps you reflect on your journey. They listen, ask the right questions, and provide insight when needed. They don't just offer advice—they challenge your thinking, ensuring that your choices align with your values and long-term goals.

Biblical Example: King Solomon - King Solomon was known for his wisdom, using discernment to lead his people. Counselor-type friends do the same. They speak truth, even when it's uncomfortable, and guide you toward growth.

Real-life example: Let's say, for example, you're considering a big life decision like quitting a job, ending a relationship, or starting something new. A trusted friend of yours helps you think things through by sitting with you, listening without judgment, and asking thoughtful questions like, "What's driving this decision?" or "Will this get you closer to who you want to be?" They help you reflect and make intentional, values-based choices.

Beyond these core roles, other key relationships add strength to your journey:

Mentors – Experts in your field who offer experience and industry insight.

Pastors – Spiritual leaders who provide biblical guidance.

Health Professionals – Therapists or counselors who support emotional well-being.

Spouses – Partners who balance family dynamics while supporting your ambitions.

When I started my business, my second husband's flexible schedule allowed him to stay home with our youngest son. His support gave me the freedom to build, travel, and work unpredictable hours. That kind of partnership made all the difference.

Support isn't just for launching goals—it's just as critical when facing transitions or moments of doubt. A good example of this is at the end of 2024 when I found myself at a crossroad in my business. Business had slowed significantly. Many companies cut back on professional development, and industry-wide, colleagues shared similar struggles. Our revenue dropped nearly 50%. I had placed high hopes on securing several contracts early in the year, but after losing multiple six-figure bids, it felt like I was playing catch-up.

At the same time, my health took a hit. What started as minor cold symptoms in November persisted for weeks. The cough lingered, coming and going, making travel and work difficult. Then in January, it escalated. I lost my voice, landed in urgent care, and one night, a severe coughing attack left me gasping for air. Struggling to breathe, I managed to tell my son to call 911. By the time paramedics arrived, I had stabilized, but within days, I was back in the emergency room with a 104-degree fever.

I was frustrated. I withdrew. I avoided talking to people. And I was angry at God.

But this was when my support system showed up in a big way. The moment I shared what was happening, messages and phone calls flooded in. My core people reminded me that I didn't have to navigate this alone.

At the same time, I was still deciding whether to close my business or keep it afloat. Once I recovered, I sat down with trusted friends and advisors to weigh my options. Today, I have a renewed sense of direction for my next chapter (pun intended) but I wouldn't have made it through without my support system.

Whether you're stepping into a new pursuit, working through a setback, or deciding what's next, your hero support system is vital. **YOU WERE NEVER MEANT TO DO THIS ALONE**. Surround yourself with mechanics who prepare you, Siri friends who guide you, and counselors who challenge and support your growth. Because a cord of three strands is not easily broken.

A strong support system doesn't just help you weather storms—

it also grounds you when the world tries to define success for you. When you're surrounded by people who remind you of your values, challenge your thinking, and celebrate your wins, you're far more likely to define success on your own terms—not someone else's.

Success on Your Own Terms

Success isn't one-size-fits-all—and the sooner we stop measuring it by someone else's standards, the freer we become to pursue what truly matters. Let's talk about what it really means to define success for yourself—something I unexpectedly learned from a pastor I had never met. His words shifted my perspective and reminded me that success isn't about chasing someone else's finish line—it's about finding peace with your own.

Around 2017—I can't pinpoint the exact year—I was attending church in my city. I had been a member for several years, and guest speakers often visited to share messages. One Sunday, Robert Madu, a pastor and speaker from Dallas, delivered a sermon titled "On Their Mark."

He compared life to the start of a race. When runners take their places, they line up, set their feet, and prepare for the signal: "On your mark, get set, go." But instead of focusing on our own mark, we often glance left and right, watching others. Before the race even begins, comparison creeps in.

That message hit home. I had been in business for five years and struggled with unhealthy competitiveness and excessive comparison. I saw others in my field—some younger—thriving, and I questioned if I was doing enough. That sermon forced me to rethink success and what it really meant.

Success is often overcomplicated. At its core, success is **achieving what you set out to do**. If I plan a trip and reach my destination, that's success. If I commit to working out three times a week and follow through, I've succeeded. If I miss a session, I don't label the entire goal a failure—I simply adjust my approach.

We often tie success to external measures—dollar amounts, awards, or recognition—but **true success is personal.** It's asking yourself: *"What does success look like for me? Am I chasing my own goals or someone else's? Am I spending too much of my time comparing myself to others?"* That final question helped me see a key difference: competition is good because it drives growth, but comparison is bad because it breeds insecurity and self-doubt.

Competition and Comparison

Many times, we view competition as a bad thing because it shifts our focus away from ourselves—but it's comparison that's the real villain. Competition can fuel us; comparison can deflate us. Competition pushes us to excel, while comparison traps us in envy.

In grade school, I competed in a spelling bee against my best friend. We were the final two. I don't remember the word I misspelled, but I remember losing. I was happy for her, but I was also envious. I started comparing my abilities to hers—grades, dance moves, singing skills, you name it. And instead of making me more ambitious, using healthy competition to make me better, it made me more envious. When we let comparison take over, it can impede how far you will succeed. And you want to succeed on your terms, in your own way, and without compromising what matters most — and in this case it was friendship.

Ambitious individuals either use competition to elevate their game or use comparison to overshadow their own progress. The wrong mindset can drain motivation and make success feel hollow. Ask yourself:

- Am I using ambition to grow or to prove something to others?

- Is my drive coming from purpose—or from pressure to keep up?

When I started my business, I partnered with a colleague who had already built a seven-figure company. He was highly successful, booked months in advance, and constantly busy. At first, I was curious—even envious—about how he secured so much business.

Then I heard about his schedule. He worked every day, morning to night, with little time for rest. Suddenly, I realized: I don't want that life.

We were in completely different seasons. This was his second business, but my first. His children were grown, while mine were still at home. He had an established client base, while I was still building mine. Neither of us was right or wrong—we were just different.

I had to decide how much time I was willing to invest in my business without sacrificing time with my children. That was my personal success metric, and I wasn't willing to compromise it.

No one else can define success for you. Take a moment to reflect on your personal success metric and write down:

- What does success look like for me?

- How do I turn competition into motivation instead of resentment?

- How am I measuring success—and does that measurement align with my values?

Success isn't about keeping up with others. It's about staying on your mark.

Faithful ambition isn't just about setting goals—it's about standing firm in what matters most. It's about taking action without compromising integrity, leaning into faith when the path ahead is unclear, and surrounding yourself with the right support. You were never meant to walk this journey alone. Your faith is your compass. Your people are your hero support. Your ambition should align with purpose, not just success.

So, take the next step. Move forward with confidence. And remember—when you build your life on faith, you're never lost. You're always exactly where you're meant to be.

ABOUT TIANA SANCHEZ

Tiana Sanchez is a powerhouse in the world of leadership development—a best-selling author, award-winning executive coach, and the CEO and Founder of TSI, LLC, a Certified Woman Business Enterprise and Woman-Owned  Small Business. With over a decade of experience as a corporate trainer and business consultant, Tiana has helped transform the way leaders lead—infusing every workshop, keynote, and boardroom with clarity, courage, and compassion.

Recognized on platforms like KTLA Morning News for her insights on workplace empathy, Tiana leads Tiana Sanchez International, home of the award-winning "Best Executive Coaching" program by HR.com. Her impact spans Fortune 500 companies, nonprofits, universities, and government agencies—with client partnerships including Mercedes Benz R&D, Warner Records, The University of Washington, Sempra Energy, Health-Ade Kombucha, and more.

Tiana's diverse background in retail, food and beverage, and finance grounds her work in real-world experience. Through tailored leadership programs, employee engagement strategies, and pulse surveys, she helps organizations build people-first cultures rooted in responsibility and results.

A #1 best-selling author of Undefeatable: Conquering Self-Defeat, F'd Up: The Upside of Failure, and contributing author of the Amazon best-seller The New C-Suite: Civil Leadership in Action, Tiana is also the voice behind a globally recognized podcast that inspires leaders around the world.

In Faith, Friendships, and Business, Tiana brings her unwavering commitment to sustainable, spirit-led leadership—proving that success isn't just about performance, but purpose. Her mission? To challenge, champion, and equip leaders to rise, lead well, and leave a legacy that matters.

Bold Moves and Beliefs Matter

By Dr. Katie W. Chu

I am not just a Survivor. I am a Conqueror.

Looking back over my life, I now see — with eyes wide open and a heart full of gratitude — that every trial, every hardship, and every tear was part of God's divine plan for my journey. Through it all, my faith became the bridge between brokenness and hope. Like the mythical phoenix, I rose from the ashes, not by my own strength, but through the unstoppable power of God's love. Today, I stand renewed, a living testimony that our God is faithful. And He is so very good.

My story didn't begin the day I was born — it was shaped long before, through generations of struggle and survival. My mother's journey became my foundation. As a young girl in China, separated from her siblings during the Communist Revolution, she endured the pain of a family torn apart and the cruelty of abuse within her own home. Yet even from that brokenness, a fierce resilience rose up—and that spirit became part of my inheritance.

This legacy of faith and perseverance taught me that Bold Moves are often born from broken places. They require more than strength—they demand trust in a God who turns ashes into beauty.

Throughout life, faith, friendship, and business often intersect in unexpected ways. It's in these intersections that we find the courage to make Bold Moves and the conviction to stand firm in the Beliefs that shape who we are.

As professionals, we constantly navigate the complexities of careers, relationships, and personal values. And when these areas meet at pivotal moments, we are called to respond—with courage, clarity, and faith. These are the moments that lead to transformation, where we emerge renewed in strength, purpose, and deeper trust in the God who guides us forward.

This is the heart of my story — the call to every believer standing at the crossroads of ambition and faith: to trust God with every move, every belief, and every new beginning. Because you are not just meant to survive. In Christ, you are called to conquer.

BELIEFS MATTER: THE CORNERSTONE OF BOLD MOVES

Bold Moves are not reckless decisions or impulsive actions. They are intentional steps of faith, made with courage and rooted in conviction. They happen when we dare to trust God more than our fears, stepping out even when the path ahead is uncertain. Bold Moves stretch us beyond comfort and into purpose, requiring us to lean wholly on His promises rather than our own understanding.

Beliefs are the foundation of every Bold Move. Without deeply rooted Beliefs — in God's goodness, in His promises, in our worth through Him — our actions would crumble under pressure. Belief fuels action: it empowers individuals to rise beyond limitations and to embrace the unknown with peace. It reminds us that while we may not always see the way, we know the One who leads us.

As Deuteronomy 31:6 reminds us: *"Be strong and courageous. Do not be afraid or terrified because of them, for the Lord your God goes with you; He will never leave you nor forsake you."*

In life's darkest times, faith does not waver — it becomes the strength that lifts us to rise again.

The Fire That Refines

Belief is more than comfort—it is the fire that refines us and the divine spark that elevates us beyond trials. Scripture promises us in Isaiah 43:2: *"When you pass through the waters, I will be with you; and when you pass through the rivers, they will not sweep over you. When you walk through the fire, you will not be burned; the flames will not set you ablaze."*

True belief is tested not when life is easy, but when life feels impossible. It is during these challenging moments that we are shaped, strengthened, and prepared for greater things. Bold Moves are born from this refining process—where faith is no longer just a feeling, but a foundation.

We rise from hardship with conviction—renewed by grace and driven by the courage to move forward with purpose. Belief reveals that every hardship serves a greater purpose, shaping us into who we are called to be. Though the path may lead through fire, we are never alone. God strengthens and guides us. Our faith gives us wings to rise, ensuing grace lifts us after every fall.

Bold Moves and Beliefs matter because they are the heartbeat of transformation. They are how we rise. They are how we walk boldly into the life God has designed just for us.

From Brokenness to Boldness

My early years bore scars that ran deeper than the surface—etched not only on my body but into my spirit. The pain, the trauma, and the silence told the story of a childhood shaped by a mother who had known only brokenness. Her own suffering, steeped in loss, became a cycle passed down to her children. But even in that darkness, something within me whispered that there had to be more.

Survival became my reality. The confusion of being unloved, the loneliness of feeling unseen, and the relentless unpredictability of my world became my norm. Yet through it all, one truth remained—I believed my life had a purpose. I didn't know what that purpose was, but I knew it existed. Faith allowed me to look beyond the immediate pain, to glimpse a future beyond the hardship. At just five years old, I made a quiet yet resolute decision: I would redefine my possibilities.

Looking back, I see more than hardship—I see resilience. Every cruel moment of adversity became a point of transformation. I didn't just survive; I chose to rise and conquer. My worth was not defined by the abuse I endured, but by the strength placed within me. *"To bestow on them a crown of beauty instead of ashes, the oil of joy instead of mourning, and a garment of praise instead of a spirit of despair."* – Isaiah 61:3

Belief, for me, was never just an idea—it was the quiet force that carried me through. It reminded me that I was part of something greater, that my life was not a mistake but a calling. *"And we know that in all things God works for the good of those who love Him, who have been called according to His purpose."* – Romans 8:28

BREAKING CYCLES, BUILDING PURPOSE

On November 1, 2001, a Bold Move was made that would forever change the course of not only my life, but my children's lives as well.

The answer became clear—it was time to rise. For the sake of my two young children, I could no longer accept the cycle of abuse that had followed me from childhood into adulthood. My husband's arrest for workplace violence forced me to confront the reality I had long ignored. The time had come to break free. Without hesitation, I reached out for help, filed for a restraining order, and took the first steps toward ending a marriage that had controlled every part of my existence.

Years of emotional and physical abuse had brought me to a pivotal moment: Would I continue to live in fear, or would I reclaim my life? The road ahead was filled with setbacks, doubts, and wounds that refused to fade overnight. But with each small step, I reclaimed a piece of myself. Every day, I chose to believe I was worth fighting for—that my story was not one of destruction, but of renewal.

Life's defining moments rarely come from places of comfort. They come when we stand at a crossroads, faced with a choice—to remain bound by fear or to step forward in faith. True strength is not the absence of fear but the willingness to act despite it, trusting that even uncertain steps are guided by a greater hand.

FROM BREAKDOWN TO BREAKTHROUGH

I boldly stepped into the unknown—not as a wife, but as a single mother. Not as someone controlled, but as someone determined to build something new. At that time, I had a small optometry practice in Rosemead, California, and just $600 to my name. My husband had controlled everything—our finances, our decisions, even my sense of worth. Suddenly, it was all on me.

With no formal business training, the challenges felt overwhelming. But I did know one thing: how to care for people. That became my foundation. Day by day, I showed up for my patients, pouring not only into the work, but into every person who walked through my doors. What began as a desperate attempt to survive slowly turned into something more—a place of healing, growth, and restoration.

Even in the ashes of what once was, God was already planting seeds for what could be. I wasn't just rebuilding a business. I was rebuilding a life. The journey taught me a truth I carry with me in every decision and every challenge since—when we entrust even the broken pieces to Him, He can build something stronger, more meaningful, and more beautiful than we ever imagined.

Moving Forward with Purpose

Caring for my patients was the one thing I could control because it felt natural. The medical side of my practice, especially contact lenses, became my refuge. But the retail side—the optical—felt overwhelming. I had no background in sales or marketing, yet the success of my practice depended on it. With no clear roadmap, I leaned on my faith, trusting that if I was meant to build something lasting, I would be guided through the process.

I came to understand that my role wasn't just about selling eyewear—it was about instilling value to an underserved community of Asian and Hispanic immigrants. Believing in the worth of my patients meant showing them the importance of their eye health. Every conversation became an opportunity, not just to fit a pair of lenses, but to affirm that they deserved the best care possible. In helping others see clearly, I was also learning to see my own worth.

A New Fire: A Personal Battle for Self-Worth

At the age of 44, I was diagnosed with breast cancer. The journey that followed was filled with trials, pain, and the profound challenge of rediscovering myself. A double mastectomy left me not only physically altered but deeply questioning my identity as a woman. Who was I without this part of me? Would I still be desirable? Would I still be me? The scars, both visible and invisible, became constant reminders of a battle fought and won—but at a cost.

Growing up as a child of abuse, self-worth always felt like something just out of reach. Facing cancer years later unearthed those old scars, shaking my sense of identity, femininity, and place in the world. But instead of retreating, I made Bold Moves. I confronted the pain, stood my ground, and chose to rewrite the narrative. I didn't just survive cancer; I conquered it by reclaiming my life with intention. I came to realize that my worth was never defined by what was taken from me, but by the strength, resilience, and relentless courage that have always been mine.

To those who have faced similar struggles—who have looked in the mirror and felt unrecognizable—I say this: You are more than your scars. You are more than the battles you have fought. You are a testament to survival, a living reflection of grace. God does not make mistakes. He rebuilds, He renews, and He refines. *"He gives beauty for ashes, the oil of joy for mourning, and the garment of praise for the spirit of heaviness."* – Isaiah 61:3 We are not broken; we are reborn.

There are seasons in life when loss and change feel too heavy to carry. When the future seems blurred by grief and uncertainty. And yet, even in those dark places, there is a quiet strength calling us forward—an invitation to rise, to rebuild, and to live with purpose. This is not about merely surviving. It's about reclaiming your life and redefining your story.

The mirror became an enemy, a cruel reminder of what had been lost. Scars that ran across skin carried a weight far beyond their physical form. It wasn't just a body that had changed—it was an identity. The loss of breasts felt like the loss of femininity, of beauty and of self-love.

And yes, there was guilt. Guilt that gripped me as I mourned for my daughters, fearing they had watched me suffer without the mother they needed. Guilt for my patients, wondering if I had left them without the care they relied on. But God, in His mercy, reminded me of Matthew 6:26: *"Look at the birds of the air; they do not sow or reap or store away in barns, and yet your heavenly Father feeds them. Are you not much more valuable than they?"* He had not called me to carry every burden alone. He was holding them, just as He was holding me.

Reclaiming Strength

After my mastectomy, it took me ten years to find the courage to make another BOLD MOVE—to simply stand in front of a mirror and truly see myself. That moment was more than just reflection—it was confrontation. Acknowledging what had changed, I had to accept that my body, no matter how altered, was still mine. Still strong. Still capable.

True transformation rarely happens in comfort. It is forged in the fire of fear, in the depths of uncertainty and vulnerability. But the harder battle came next: believing that my scars don't define my worth. There was grief for what had been lost, but also a quiet realization of what had been gained. Strength. Resilience.

A deeper understanding of existence beyond the physical. Healing was not just about the body; it was about rebuilding an identity no longer tethered to society's definition of beauty. It was about understanding that worth had never been tied to any one part of me—it had always been whole.

The Role of Daughters' Love

No one walks through fire alone. In the midst of self-doubt and silent suffering, it was the voices of others that broke through the haze. Friends who refused to let sorrow take root. Loved ones who reminded me that worth had never been dependent on physical perfection. The presence of those who saw beyond the scars and reflected back strength instead of pity—that was the lifeline.

My daughters became the mirror that showed what was difficult to see alone. Their unwavering love slowly replaced worthlessness. It was through their eyes that new confidence began to take shape. Their words, their encouragement, their unrelenting insistence that wholeness had never been lost—this became the foundation upon which a new sense of beauty was built.

"Children are a heritage from the Lord, offspring a reward from him." – Psalm 127:3

Their love didn't just comfort me—it became God's reminder that I am blessed, that healing is possible, and that His gifts often come through the very people who love us most.

BOLD MOVES: NEW PERSPECTIVES

The cancer journey did not end with acceptance. It became a mission to redefine beauty, to challenge the narrative that scars were something to hide. It became a declaration that survival was not just about making it through—it was about thriving. It was about making bold choices, taking up space, and living fully in a body that had fought to be here. It means living in the present. This transformation extended beyond personal healing. It seeped into work, into relationships, into every interaction.

In business, it became a drive to create a space where others could see their own worth reflected back at them. Patients walked through the door carrying their own battles, their own insecurities. And in them, there was recognition. If they could be reminded of their value, if they could walk away feeling just a little more seen, a little more worthy, then every struggle had been worth it.

When I left an abusive marriage, it was a Bold Move—a leap of faith into the unknown. Building a business from nothing was another, driven by trust in myself and a vision no one else could see. Facing cancer became the ultimate surrender to God's will. Choosing the double mastectomy felt like losing a part of myself. Yet in that loss, I discovered a new kind of strength. Each Bold Move didn't just help me survive—it shaped who I am. I rose, transformed by the very trials that tried to consume me.

Believe in You, Believe in God

Life's defining moments are not made in a single instant. They are a series of choices made every day—to stand tall, to silence the voices of doubt, to reclaim joy. The scars remain, but they are no longer symbols of loss. They are testaments to survival, to strength, to a life that refuses to be defined by pain.

The journey is ongoing, but one truth has become clear: worth was never in question. It had always been there, unshaken by change, untouched by scars. And with each step forward, that truth becomes easier to believe.

Our Professional Lives of Ministry

In my own career, I discovered that faith and work are not separate forces but deeply intertwined. Becoming an optometrist was never just a career choice; it was a calling—a ministry. Through my profession, I had the privilege to serve, extend compassion, and reflect the same grace God showed me in my darkest moments. *"Commit to the Lord whatever you do, and He will establish your plans."* – Proverbs 16:3

Bold Moves are not confined to personal struggles; they shape our professional journeys as well. The work we do—the platforms we stand on—can become vessels for meaningful impact. Success is not just about financial gain or status; it is about living out our purpose in a way that honors God. *"Whatever you do, work at it with all your heart, as working for the Lord, not for human masters."* – Colossians 3:23

Whether mentoring, providing care for those in need, or

empowering others, my practice became more than a business—it became a mission to live out my convictions. Embracing the greater purpose God has designed for us, every professional interaction became an opportunity to share His love. *"Let your light shine before others, that they may see your good deeds and glorify your Father in heaven."* – Matthew 5:16

Breaking Free: A Mindset Shift of Faith and Bold Moves

For over 25 years, my business carried a quiet disconnect. While my contact lens practice thrived, the optical side remained stagnant—frozen in time. Patients received exceptional care through eye health evaluations, yet when it came to selecting eyewear, the focus stayed fixed on affordability. This stood in stark contrast to the premium options I confidently offered in contact lenses.

I assumed high-end eyewear was of no interest to my patients—until a vendor consultant posed one simple but powerful question: **"If you confidently offer premium contact lenses, why not do the same with fashion eyewear and ophthalmic lens options?"**

That question opened my eyes in a way I hadn't anticipated. My hesitation wasn't about finances or fear of change—it was an unspoken belief I had carried for years without realizing it. I assumed my patients would only choose what was practical, never imagining they might long for something more. But the truth was, they trusted me—not only with their eye health, but with their confidence, their identity, and how they saw themselves.

They were looking to me for guidance—for permission to aspire to something greater. And I was just beginning to understand the role I had been given in that journey.

The consultant didn't just introduce new products or pricing strategies. She offered a new lens through which to see possibility. Together, we reimagined the optical space, introduced premium luxury eyewear, and transformed the entire patient experience.

But the shift went far deeper than a business decision—it became an act of faith. Her words, *"Let's take it in baby steps,"* became more than practical advice. They were grace-filled reminders to trust the process and move forward with courage. She became a kind of guardian angel, gently helping me dismantle old fears and replace them with faith.

As my perspective changed, so did the way I saw my patients. No longer simply customers, they became individuals deserving of beauty, dignity, and excellence. And as I extended that belief to them, God began showing me how to extend it to myself.

I am worthy of excellence—in business, in relationships, and in life—because God created me for more. He calls us not just to survive, but to thrive.

And every Bold Move we make in faith brings us one step closer to the life He's always had in mind for us.

A Space of Healing and Renewal

For years, the optical side of my practice symbolized an older chapter of my life—a chapter marked by broken dreams and unhealed wounds. Redesigning it wasn't just about updating aesthetics; it became a deeply personal act of healing. It was a Bold Move toward wholeness.

After four months of constructing elegant, French-inspired wood cabinetry, I layered in my love for Shabby Chic design. Chandeliers sparkled above a plush white shag rug in the waiting area, infusing the space with warmth and light. Every detail spoke of renewal—a fresh start, a new identity not just for *Katie* or *Dr. Chu*, but for me— the fully empowered, beautifully integrated woman God had always seen.

This space became more than a business. It became a sanctuary— a place where both my patients and I could find healing, hope, and restoration.

Every touch, every carefully chosen decor, whispered of new

beginnings—of a woman reclaiming her voice, her dreams, and her worth. And during this entire process, I had no fear. God was with me. He never abandoned me. He never stopped loving me.

A New Beginning: A Spiritual Awakening

This journey of transformation was never just about business growth—it has always been, and continues to be, a deep spiritual awakening.

Each Bold Move I make calls for faith: the faith to take risks, the faith to trust, and the faith to believe in the unseen work God is doing within me.

And as I am transformed, so are the lives of those who walk through my doors. Patients who arrive feeling unsure in life often leave not only with clearer vision, but with renewed confidence, dignity, and hope.

My practice is more than a place for optometric services—it has become a sanctuary. A peaceful, welcoming space where hearts are uplifted and people are reminded of their immeasurable worth. Because when people feel truly seen—when they enter a space that reflects their value and affirms who they are—they don't just leave with improved vision. They leave believing they were made for more.

Success of my business is no longer defined by sales or statistics. It's measured by lives touched, hope rekindled, and Beliefs that take root in souls longing for purpose.

Rising from the Ashes: A Conqueror

Through abuse, cancer, guilt, and fear—I see God's fingerprints all over my story. He was never absent, never silent. He was refining me, preparing me for something greater.

I move forward not as a survivor of my past but as a conqueror refined by fire. My scars do not symbolize loss; they are testimonies of resurrection. I am not defined by what I have endured but by the woman I have become.

To anyone standing in the ashes, wondering if life can bloom from brokenness—hear this: You are not forsaken. You are being prepared. The fire is not your end; it is the beginning of your rise. In Christ, we always rise.

WHEN WORK BECOMES A CALLING: A LIFE TRANSFORMED

Life's cycles of joy and hardship shape us, but when embraced with faith, community, and purpose, they transform us into who we were always meant to be. *"For I know the plans I have for you,"* declares the Lord, *"plans to prosper you and not to harm you, plans to give you hope and a future."* - Jeremiah 29:11

I realize that every pivotal step in my journey—whether in business or life—was never just about success. It was about healing, faith, and creating a space where others feel seen, heard, and valued. God didn't just give me a business; He gave me a mission—to build something that reflects His love. When belief guides our work, it transcends a job and becomes a calling.

A COMMUNITY OF FAITH, STRENGTH, AND SUPPORT

No one rises alone. God places people in our lives to offer strength, encouragement, and wisdom. My journey would not have been possible without the unconditional support of faith-filled friends, family, and mentors. *"As iron sharpens iron, so one person sharpens another."* - Proverbs 27:17)

True community, rooted in faith, is a source of unshakable

resilience. Together, we stand strong through life's fiercest battles. Their prayers sustain us in moments of weakness, and their steadfast belief in God's goodness reminds us that hope is never lost. *"Therefore encourage one another and build each other up, just as in fact you are doing."* – 1 Thessalonians 5:11

Daughters' Bold Moves of Sacrifice and Purpose

This same foundation of faith and support has shaped my daughters, guiding them as they step into their own callings. Their lives are testaments to the power of trusting God's plan—even when it leads them down unexpected paths. Each has embraced her purpose with courage, demonstrating that true strength often begins with a Bold Move: the willingness to surrender fully to His will.

One of the greatest lessons I've learned about faith and purpose comes from my daughter Codi, a United States Marine Corps officer. Her calling was undeniable—delivered through a dream in which God placed the desire in her heart to serve. She felt His guidance to protect the freedoms and democracy that make America a refuge for so many. Knowing that God had planted this purpose within her was both humbling and awe-inspiring. It reinforced the power of trusting His plan, even when it differs from what we imagined for ourselves.

The night she left for Officer Candidates School in Quantico, VA, was one of the most emotional moments of my life. Sitting across from her at a restaurant, she looked at me and said, *"Mom, if today's my last day on earth, I need you to know that I am good."* Her words filled me with an unshakable peace, as if God Himself were speaking through her—reminding me that no matter what happens, she is ready. And more importantly, that I, too, must embrace each day with purpose, just as she follows her calling with faith and courage. *"Have I not commanded you? Be strong and courageous. Do not be afraid; do not be discouraged, for the Lord your God will be with you wherever you go."* – Joshua 1:9

That same unwavering trust in God's plan is reflected in my older daughter, Bailee, who has carved her own path in the sports industry, negotiating marketing deals for NFL players. In a field defined by fierce competition, stepping into that space requires confidence, resilience, and an unshakable belief in one's abilities. Her determination to succeed in such a high-stakes environment is a testament to her strength and perseverance—qualities I deeply admire. She, too, teaches me what it means to trust in God's direction, to keep moving forward even when the path is uncertain. *"I can do all things through Christ who strengthens me."* – Philippians 4:13

Both of my daughters have chosen careers that involve both offense and defense—strategic decisions that determine outcomes. But no matter which side you're on, success requires balance, teamwork, and trust in a greater plan.

Through their experiences, I have deepened my own walk with God. Their Bold Moves of faith—their willingness to say yes to His calling and to stand firm in uncertainty—have inspired me to trust more fully, to step forward with courage, and to believe that God's dreams for us are always greater than we dare to imagine.

Every step they take—every defining choice they make—is more than just a decision; it is a living example of transformation. It is a reminder that when we trust God enough to make Bold Moves, He not only directs our paths, but He also reshapes our hearts, our futures, and our very sense of purpose.

Their journeys call each of us to lean deeper into faith, to move forward even when the road is unclear, and to believe that true transformation begins the moment we choose to trust Him with everything we are.

PHOENIX MOM: EMPOWERING THE NEXT GENERATION

Parenting wasn't about being a *"Tiger Mom"*—the overbearing, controlling force that pushes children toward success at any cost. Instead, I embraced the role of a *"Phoenix Mom"*—strong and disciplined, yet always allowing my children the freedom to explore, grow, and soar. I never clipped their wings; instead, I was their wind, lifting them higher, guiding them, and standing steadfast by their side—just as God does for us.

"Like an eagle that stirs up its nest and hovers over its young, that spreads its wings to catch them and carries them aloft." – Deuteronomy 32:11

This philosophy shaped not just my parenting but also the way I ran my business. I cultivated an environment where my patients could flourish, where they could see themselves as deserving of the best—not just in their vision, but in their lives. I extended this same approach to my staff, instilling in them the values of listening, compassion, and trust. We are all capable of more than we imagine, and when we align our Beliefs with action, we unlock possibilities beyond our wildest dreams.

LEAVING A LEGACY

Lasting transformation begins with bold decisions rooted in conviction. Through faith, community, and the work we dedicate our lives to, we build more than businesses—we build legacies. Our work is not just transactional; it's deeply relational. When we lead with trust and belief, we earn genuine loyalty—not only from patients but from everyone we serve.

The transformation of my practice was more than a physical

renovation; it was a spiritual renewal. It became a space that reflects the true worth of every patient—a place that reminds them they are beautiful, valuable, and deserving of life's best. While the streets around us bear signs of struggle, with abandoned buildings and graffiti, the heart of this community shines with strength. That is what my practice celebrates: the resilience, dignity, and beauty within the people it serves.

The Spirit of Touch Points

The risks we take—whether in our careers, relationships, or personal growth—are never just about us. They are part of something greater, aligned with the purpose God has placed in our hearts. In life, there are moments—**Touch Points**—when we feel a deep stirring, an undeniable pull toward something that defies logic or comfort. That is the Spirit of God urging us to have faith, to trust in Him. *"Trust in the Lord with all your heart and lean not on your own understanding; in all your ways submit to Him, and He will make your paths straight."* – Proverbs 3:5-6

No more hesitations. No more "BUT's" or "IF's"—Just Do It. Make that Bold Move.

Trust Him. Believe in Him. *"For we live by faith, not by sight."* – 2 Corinthians 5:7

God has already paved the way for you to rise.

Hope, Purpose, and Meaning

Move forward with faith, trusting that God is with you every step of the way. Your story matters—and your impact will ripple far beyond your lifetime. As you walk this path, hold fast to your Beliefs, knowing that through faith, friendships, and your work, you are shaping a legacy that will endure.

Faith, friendship, and purpose are not just guiding ideals—they are the foundation of a life well-lived. Through them, we don't just survive hardship—we rise above it. *"No, in all these things we are more than conquerors through Him who loved us."* – Romans 8:37 So take each step with confidence, anchored in faith. Trust that your journey holds meaning far beyond what you can see today.

Embracing the Call to Rise: Your Bold Move Awaits

Every scar, every struggle, and every sleepless night was never the end of my story—it was preparation. God was crafting a greater plan all along. Each setback built my resilience. Each loss made room for something more. And through it all, faith became the steady force that lifted me from brokenness into boldness, from ashes into beauty. I didn't just rise—I rose stronger, wiser, and anchored in purpose.

My journey is a testimony to the power of Bold Moves and the unshakable truth that our Beliefs shape everything. Whatever fire you're walking through, remember this: you are not alone. God is already preparing the way, even when you can't yet see it. So be encouraged: Whatever you face today, you were created to overcome. Step forward in faith. Embrace the unknown with open hands. Rise into the purpose God has prepared for you.

THE MOMENT OF DECISION

We all come to a defining moment—the choice to remain in the ashes or to rise. God's promise is clear: He brings beauty from brokenness and purpose from pain. You are not defined by your struggles; you are refined by them. And through this refining, your true purpose is revealed.

"Consider it pure joy, my brothers and sisters, whenever you face trials of many kinds, because you know that the testing of your faith produces perseverance." – James 1:2-3

Your moment is now.

What Bold Move is God calling you to make today?

About Dr. Katie W. Chu OD

Dr. Katie W. Chu is a trailblazing optometrist, national speaker, and compassionate healer who brings nearly 30 years of vision care, heart, and hope to the Rosemead immigrant community. A first-generation American-born Chinese, Dr. Chu carries forward a remarkable 160-year family legacy that began with her ancestors' work on the Transcontinental Railroad in 1864—a testament to perseverance, purpose, and the pursuit of the American dream.

With degrees from UCLA and the Southern California College of Optometry, Dr. Chu is known for blending clinical excellence with genuine compassion. Her practice is rooted in cutting-edge technology, premium eye care products, and a patient-first philosophy that centers kindness, respect, and dignity. As a breast cancer survivor, she brings a deep level of empathy and personal strength into every patient encounter—especially for those walking through their own health journeys.

Beyond her clinic, Dr. Chu is a sought-after speaker and consultant in the optometry world, frequently invited to share her insights at national conferences and in respected industry publications. Her expertise and passion have made her a trusted voice in both professional circles and her local community.

But perhaps her proudest role is being "Mom." A devoted mother to two accomplished daughters—one a senior marketing manager for NFL players, the other a Marine Corps officer with a master's degree in engineering—Dr. Chu's legacy is one of vision, leadership, and unwavering love.

In Faith, Friendships, and Business, Dr. Chu shares her story as a reminder that clarity—both in sight and in life—starts from within. Her life's mission is to help others see more clearly, lead more boldly, and live more purposefully, no matter where they're starting from.

Grace-Filled Leadership

By Brittany Emery

Grace-Filled Leadership Starts with a Grace-Filled Life

I've been in leadership for over a decade now—long enough to know that leading is both a privilege and a challenge. I've led in ministry, worked in secular spaces, and had my fair share of both failures and successes. I've learned that leadership isn't about having all the right answers or doing everything perfectly—it's about growth, humility, and grace.

Early in my journey, I thought leadership had more to do with confidence, strategy, and knowledge. But over the years, I've discovered that grace is one of the most essential qualities a leader can embody. In my experiences as a manager in customer service and leader in full-time ministry, I've encountered my share of people with unique personalities and qualities. After experiencing various challenges that come with being a part of the people business - having the greatest strategies, more knowledge, and being self-assured did not help me overcome all the challenges. Grace is what carries you through your shortcomings, sustains you in difficult seasons, and allows you to lead others with wisdom and compassion.

So, where does grace come in? Who does it come from? And how can we give it freely? I'm both a recipient of more grace than I could ever deserve and someone who strives to extend it to others. That's why I'm excited to unpack this topic with you. Because grace-filled leadership doesn't start with a title or position—it starts with a grace-filled life.

To begin, let's look at what it really means to be filled with grace. The Bible makes it clear: grace isn't something we earn, achieve, or manufacture. It is owned, derived, and gifted by God.

Ephesians 2:8 (ESV) says, *"For by grace you have been saved through faith. And this is not your own doing; it is the gift of God."* There is no amount of money, no title, no degree, no asset, no investment portfolio, or hours of overtime work that could afford us grace by our own doing. It is simply God's gift to us.

Many believers are likely familiar with 2 Corinthians 12:9: *"But he said to me, 'My grace is sufficient for you, for my power is made perfect in weakness.' Therefore, I will boast all the more gladly of my weaknesses, so that the power of Christ may rest upon me."* Notice how grace and power are described in this verse as belonging to God. God is both the giver, and the maker of this gift called grace.

That means our limitations—our weaknesses, our failures, our uncertainties—don't disqualify us. Instead, they create space for God's grace to work through us.

To make this clearer, I'll share with you what grace is and what grace isn't:

Grace is a gift that is freely given. Grace is not earned and does not come with IOU contingencies attached.

Grace is emotional and spiritual generosity. Grace is not keeping score or withholding love based on someone's shortcomings or failures; it flows from a place of compassion.

Grace empowers growth. Grace does not keep us stagnant or excuse wrongdoing; it invites transformation from the inside out, giving us strength to do better.

Grace gives second chances. Grace is not limited to a single opportunity; it offers restoration.

Grace allows for a positive impact. Grace-filled leadership is not to be a leader without boundaries or to simply allow people to walk all over you.

Grace offers freedom. Grace does not trap us in guilt or shame; it frees us to live with hope and possibility, even after failure.

A Life Filled with Grace: The Power of Giving What's Undeserved

Most people give gifts with the expectation that they will be used. There's thought, purpose, and meaning behind them. Grace is the same way—it's been given to us in abundance, and it's our honor (and let's be straight-forward, our responsibility) to use it well.

In all my years working and serving alongside people, I've met every kind of personality—cheerful ones, difficult ones, wounded ones, wise ones, and of course, there's me: the chief needer of God's grace.

Case in point: years ago, I was at a graduation ceremony in Pomona, CA. That day, I was more distracted than I'd like to admit. After the ceremony, I joined the masses trying to escape a five-story parking structure. To keep myself from losing patience in the never-ending traffic, I was deep in conversation on the phone.

Finally, I reached the exit, and just as I was about to leave—I bumped the car in front of me. Not once, not twice—but three times. Back-to-back. I was so shocked by my own mistake that instead of stopping immediately, I kept tapping the poor stranger's bumper like we were playing bumper cars.

The woman got out of her car, and she was not thrilled. Rightfully so. I was a distracted young adult, chatting away on the phone instead of paying attention. Her voice was sharp *"How did you even do that?!"* and I stood there, heart racing, knowing full well my dad, who was covering the car insurance at the time, was definitely going to kill me.

But then, something unexpected happened. Her frustration softened. She looked at me and asked, *"Are you okay?"* She listened to my flustered apologies, took a deep breath, and instead of calling the cops, the insurance company, or my dad—she chose grace. She decided to let me off the hook. She didn't request my information, she didn't make any insurance claims, nothing.

I didn't deserve her grace. She had every right to escalate the situation. But she let it go. And looking back, I realize that grace didn't just benefit me—it likely benefited her too. By choosing grace, she saved herself from unnecessary stress, paperwork, and an afternoon spent dealing with all the antics that come with an accident. In the grand scheme of things, it wasn't worth it. Thankfully, her bumper was not at all damaged.

That's the thing about grace. It's a gift—one that favorably changes both the giver and the receiver.

Leading with grace will not always be the simplest choice. Sometimes it costs an attitude here, ego there, and especially impacts your humility. Maybe you've never had to make the choice to choose grace because someone hit your car 3 times in a row, but you will more than likely run into an instance whether at church, at work, in business, or home, where grace will be required of you. Allow me to share some ways to help you make the right choice.

Grace in Action: Navigating Leadership with Wisdom and Conviction

For leaders, there are more opportunities that arise to give grace than we often realize. Leadership doesn't only come with a title and position, but it also has the responsibility to the people it influences. You may have inherited a leadership position, or you are looking to grow into one. Regardless of your role we owe the people that we lead (our families, colleagues, team members) the dignity of doing things with integrity and humility.

Operating with grace can look like confronting an issue head on, having hard conversations, all while maintaining a high level of emotional maturity. It can also look like choosing to walk in the fruit of the Spirit (love, joy, peace, patience, kindness, gentleness, self-control, goodness, and faithfulness), and putting the needs of others above your own.

If I am honest there are many times in my leadership that my first thought was to complain about something or someone before grace even crossed my mind. Interestingly enough, the majority of my complaints and concerns have first been resolved through prayer before I ever witnessed them resolved in person.

When I initially got started in full time ministry, I was trying to learn and figure out my footing. There were leaders that had gone before me, to do the work and roles similar to mine. People would have been used to their leadership and not mine. I'm certain at that time, I would have led pretty self-consciously.

I believe I felt self-conscious because I wasn't sure if I could amount to the previous leadership expectations and I was doubtful about my ability to influence people. As months passed, I started to focus too much on what others were doing and how they led. I could feel the pressure of comparison and self-doubt build up within me. With pressure mounting, I started to take my concerns to God. I would pray about the things that worried me and find comfort in the Bible. I even began showing myself grace to learn and develop in my own ways.

The barriers that I had built up began to loosen. This is the gift of grace in action. As God was gracing me in my leadership, I was also learning how necessary it is to give yourself grace as you enter new seasons and chapters in life.

The Grace Filter: Leading with Accountability

A good leader will create for themselves a powerful filtering system, much like a water filter that removes impurities and contaminants to make water safe and pure. Similarly, a grace filter helps leaders sift through challenges, biases, and emotional reactions, allowing them to lead with wisdom, compassion, and accountability, maximizing their leadership impact in a way that benefits "everyone they lead." Healthy filtering systems can take different forms: seeking wise counsel that holds you accountable in both heart and conduct, learning from coaches or leaders, and regularly examining your thoughts, decisions, and actions.

Let's look at the effectiveness of each of these filtering systems:

Wise Counsel - This refers to people that are able to speak into your life. These people offer you wisdom that helps you to be a better spouse, parent, leader, entrepreneur, student, etc. You are able to receive from them because they practice what they preach and for lack of better words, they have skin in the game. You may have wise counsel that sticks with you throughout your life journey and in other instances you'll have wise counsel that is only prominent in a particular season of your life.

Because their wisdom is such a gift, it's important you make great returns on the relationship by applying this wisdom. When you're dealing with a situation that you are unsure of how to handle, run it by your wise counsel. When they challenge you to show someone grace, don't take it lightly. Submit, and see how God can cover you in the places that you're submitted.

I have a friend that I have known for 10 years. Our relationship started as only acquaintances. It would just so happen that we started to serve at church together in the same ministry. As we began serving together, we grew closer, but trust was slow to grow on both of our parts.

With more time passing and more opportunities to see each other through various life stages and transitions, our friendship has grown to a place that feels extremely safe. Because of the trust and care we've shown one another over time, when she speaks, I listen and when I speak, she listens.

Every so often, as my friend feels led, I will receive a text from her with the question *"how's your heart?"*. This question to me means, *"Brittany, how well have you been forgiving people? Are you giving grace where grace is needed? Are you keeping a score count of offenses or letting things go?".* I appreciate the depth of wisdom that I gain from this friendship. I understand this type of relationship may not be true for everyone. But I advise you to have at least one-person in your life that can speak so frankly with you. The onus is on us to not only hear wisdom when it's spoken, but to do something with it.

Coaches and Leaders - Will help expand your leadership capacity. We know that not everyone can provide wise counsel for us one on one, but the beauty of today is that we can be coached anywhere. From books to podcasts or sermons, our leadership growth is infinite. I don't know that I'll ever have the opportunity to thank John Maxwell face to face for all of the leadership principles I've learned from him over time, but I get to continue being coached by him every time I open up one of his books.

When I'm feeling a nudge to dig further into my emotions and feelings, I like to listen to any of Lysa TerKeurst podcasts. She has a true gift of consulting her emotions yet trusting and honoring God with them. At this point, if we are not growing and developing in our leadership and walk of love the issue isn't a lack of knowledge, but a lack of willingness to learn.

Take Inventory of our Thoughts - When I was allowed my first opportunity to lead in the workplace, I was only 18 years old. I worked for a Californian-Mexican fast food restaurant as a busser starting at 16 years old then moved up to shift leader position a couple of years later. At that time, if you were the leader that was doing the closing shift, one of your tasks was to conclude the evening with an end of day journal entry. The journal entry would include items like, *"Busy night",* or *"We ran out of asada 30 minutes before closing",* and *"Jane Doe went above and beyond with customer service today"* or on the contrary *"John Doe ignored customers".* You get the picture.

Keeping a note of these items helped us to debrief with our store manager and look for opportunities to grow, and for areas to keep an eye on. In the same way that I kept an inventory and note of these important daily moments, I caution you that it's even more important to keep an inventory of your thoughts. We must filter our thoughts by what is important and truthful, and note our opportunities to grow.

What does this look like practically? It starts with not replaying the same negative thoughts over and over like a broken record. Our go to filter should be to fix our thoughts on *"whatever is true, whatever is honorable, whatever is just, whatever is pure, whatever is lovely, whatever is commendable, if there is any excellence, if there is anything worthy of praise"* – Philippians 4:8 (ESV). When scripture becomes your filter, grace pours out of you a lot more seamlessly. The reality is that our flesh likes to get in the way. Everything that God instructs me to do, my flesh wants to do the exact opposite.

For example, instead of thinking about what is true, my mind tends to gravitate towards what is false. As I reflect on a moment in the day where maybe I made a mistake, my mind can easily become a broken record. Repeating, *"You messed up, you're not a competent leader."* But I can change the station. I can flip it to a healthy and truthful record that says, *"Yes, you made a mistake but what can you learn from this?".* Your thoughts need clean filters in order to operate at the proper capacity. It's important that we renew our minds daily and maintain healthy thinking.

When we combine adhering to wise counsel, learning from various coaches and leaders, and taking an inventory of our thoughts, we create a strong filtering system to help us become leaders that are intentional with giving grace.

Grace Killers

Now that we've dissected some healthy ways of leading with grace, it's important that we don't forget to uncover the grace killers. There are some things that will stand in the way of you and grace-filled leadership if you are not careful. This list could be extended; however, I want to focus on the most common ways grace can die before it ever has the opportunity to live.

Gossip - *"Casual or unconstrained conversation or reports about other people, typically involving details that are not confirmed as being true."* Gossip kills grace because it focuses on what we believe to be the worst in people, rather than the best of people. It fills in the blank, where there are no words. The most unfortunate part is gossip almost always gets it wrong whereas grace often presents a right solution.

Pride - *"A high, especially an excessively high opinion of one's own worth or importance which gives rise to a feeling or attitude of superiority over others; inordinate self-esteem."* – Proverbs 16:18 paraphrased tells us that pride comes before the downfall. Therefore, the higher we lift ourselves up, the harder we fall.

Comparison - Focusing on people to your left or right rather than focusing ahead. As leaders we need to be visionaries. When our attention gets lost on what those around us are doing, we substitute God's approval of us, for man's opinion. Instead of visioning for the future, we end up stuck in the present. It's hard to lead with grace, when you have blurred vision.

Judgement - Similar to gossip, judgement has preconceived notions and or pre-existing beliefs about a person that causes us to jump to conclusions. These preconceived thoughts can taint our ability to love people well. When we are quick to judge, we often forfeit second chances and opportunities for people to get it right.

Unhealed wounds and unhealthy cycles - If I were to sum up these grace killers into one category, I'd say the commonality in all of them are unhealed wounds and unhealthy cycles. Identifying this killer will likely require both spiritual and therapeutic guidance. However, we can note that grace will never have room to grow and develop within our leadership when we have unaddressed hurts and habits in our lives.

As with our physical bodies, when a wound is not treated, it can end up getting infected. Wound infections can lead to pain, swelling, fever, and much worse when not addressed. Unfortunately, we can often worsen our emotional, spiritual, and mental condition when a wound has been neglected for long enough.

Instead of being filled with grace to lead, we'll find ourselves filled with offense, hurt, and unforgiveness. Our past experiences shape how we engage with the world, often in ways we don't immediately recognize. Unhealed wounds will influence our relationships, decision-making, and even leadership style.

I reached out to some friends with expertise in marriage and family therapy, coaching, and leadership development. Together, we created the reflection questions below. Your honest answers may reveal deeper areas in need of healing.

Do you prefer working alone rather than with others? This could stem from a fear of abandonment, leading you to recluse as a form of self-protection.

Do you allow yourself to make mistakes? If not, you may be seeking constant acceptance, believing that failure equates to rejection.

Do you find purpose in your relationships? Our connections with others are often a reflection of how we experience God's love and presence.

Do you tend to micromanage? A history of disappointment or being let down may have made you feel that control is the only way to avoid future hurt.

Are you skeptical of other people's motives? If trust feels difficult, it may be because past wounds have left you guarded and hesitant to be vulnerable.

Do you struggle to say "no"? The need to please and take on everything for everyone can be a sign of seeking validation through overextension.

Do you have difficulty trusting people? A past betrayal can create deep-rooted fears, making trust feel like a risk rather than a foundation.

Do you hesitate to ask for help? You might fear being a burden, believing that self-reliance is the safest option.

Do you feel the need to be the most competent person in the room? This could stem from wounds related to your sense of value and worth.

Do you feel compelled to provide input in every meeting? A need for acceptance may be driving your desire to always be heard.

Are you afraid to share your ideas? Fear of rejection can silence your voice before you even get a chance to speak.

Do you avoid confrontation at all costs? If you've experienced an abuse of power, you may associate confrontation with harm rather than healthy resolution.

Would you consider yourself confident? A struggle with insecurity may be keeping you from fully stepping into your identity.

Each of these questions is an invitation to self-awareness and healing. Recognizing the root of these patterns is the first step toward breaking free from them. Where do you see yourself in these reflections?

One might say, *"It's not that deep."* But the truth is, it is that deep. Scripture reminds us, *"...For the Lord sees not as man sees: man looks on the outward appearance, but the Lord looks on the heart."* – 1 Samuel 16:7 (ESV).

We can present ourselves as strong, capable, and put together, but if unhealed wounds are festering beneath the surface, they will inevitably shape how we lead and love others. If we struggle to extend grace, trust people, or walk in confidence, it's not just a leadership issue—it's a heart issue.

God is not simply after behavior modification; He's after transformation. And transformation starts with awareness. The reflections you just walked through aren't about condemnation; they're about revelation.

What is keeping you from leading from a place of wholeness? What's blocking you from being a leader who is full, overflowing, and ready to do good work? If something in you feels exposed, don't ignore it—invite God into it. Let Him do the heart work so that you can step fully into the leader He's called you to be.

When we root out these grace-killers, we make room for a leadership style that reflects the heart of God—one of love, truth, and transformation.

GRACE-FILLED LEGACY

I can only imagine my life today, had I not received grace. More importantly, as we reflect on grace-filled leadership, it's worth mentioning that the greatest instruction manual ever written, The Bible, would be missing the majority of its text if grace was absent. Paul couldn't write the majority of the New Testament without grace. Peter couldn't lead the Church and new disciples without grace. Timothy couldn't become one of the greatest yet youngest Christian leaders without grace. All of these leaders both received God's grace and freely gave it out. Our leadership has the power to redeem others through second chances.

My heart and hope is that you become a leader that can combine your faith, friendships, and business to make a powerful and transformative impact in your area of influence. Please don't overlook the grace factor. People today are at a grace deficit. Our society has been quick to cancel someone for one wrong move, one wrong word, or one wrong action. Instead of cancelling, grace multiplies.

It's never too late to start leading with grace. Start by receiving grace so that you can give it out. From there, make the choice to choose grace as your response while you navigate your leadership journey. Maintain a clean grace filter by keeping wise and trusted voices around you, consistently learning, and inventorying your thoughts and actions daily. Stay clear of the grace killers that ruin relationships and stunt your growth. Seek healing through Christ while also embracing the support of therapy. With these steps, you will leave a grace-filled legacy that endures in faith, friendships, and business.

ABOUT BRITTANY EMERY

Brittany Emery is a passionate, faith-driven leader who believes that true leadership is rooted in grace, empathy, and service. With over a decade of experience in both the marketplace and full-time ministry, Brittany brings a unique perspective to every space she enters—one that blends professionalism with purpose, and strategy with soul.

For more than eight years, Brittany has faithfully served at one of the nation's largest churches, working alongside thousands of volunteers to help them grow, lead, and thrive. Whether training team leaders, coordinating large-scale events, or offering a listening ear and timely encouragement, Brittany's heart has always been the same: to call out the gold in others and help them step into the fullness of who God created them to be.

Her gift for leadership and love for people started young. From early days of organizing community projects to leading ministry teams, Brittany has always had an eye for detail and a heart for transformation. That calling now extends into her career, where she works remotely as an administrative coordinator—supporting high-level and executive leaders with excellence, integrity, and grace. She's the behind-the-scenes strategist who ensures things run smoothly, all while keeping people at the center.

In every role she plays—whether leader, encourager, wife, or friend—Brittany shows up with quiet strength and unwavering faith. Married to her best friend since 2019, she values deep connection, intentional living, and the power of showing up fully, even in the small moments.

In Faith, Friendships, and Business, Brittany contributes her heartfelt chapter on Grace-Filled Leadership—a powerful look at how leading with compassion, humility, and faith isn't just good leadership… it's Kingdom leadership. Through her words, she encourages readers to release perfection, embrace progress, and lead others the way Christ leads us—with truth, love, and grace at the core.

Praising God While Dealing with Toxic Relationships

By La Crease Coleman

I spent 20 years in corporate healthcare, serving as a regional director overseeing five hospitals and 26 direct-report managers. My work required leading diverse teams, navigating organizational politics, and developing leaders under pressure. And while I thrived professionally, I also witnessed the darker side of leadership— gossip, manipulation, and power struggles, even among the most capable executives. Competition thrived, and tension brewed between CEOs and leadership at multiple hospitals.

Over the last 16 years I've been in ministry, I've encountered similar dysfunctional patterns—miscommunication, jealousy, and control. But I've also discovered something powerful: God uses these very moments to shape us if we let Him.

One of the most formative places for me has been missions. I started by taking foster and at-risk children on trips, and that grew into leading global outreaches for all ages. When you remove people from their comfort zones—into unfamiliar places with spiritual pressure and emotional intensity—everything surfaces. Personalities collide, emotional immaturity reveals itself, and unresolved pain can turn a mission field into a battlefield.

But even then—especially then—praise has been my weapon.

These experiences taught me that worship isn't just for Sundays. Praise has the power to shift atmospheres, silence offense, and guard our hearts in hostile environments. It realigns your focus from people to the only One who brings peace. Whether navigating a boardroom in healthcare or a prayer room on the field, I've learned no place is immune to relational strain.

One of my first up-close experiences with toxic behavior came from a direct report who aimed to become a director. Our professional relationship gradually turned into a friendship, but I noticed her advancement tactics often came at others' expense. When I addressed it, she claimed I had been handed my position and refused to acknowledge the years of sacrifice it took to get there. Her resentment eventually turned to slander. She blamed me for her mistakes, spread falsehoods, and undermined me behind closed doors.

In ministry, there's a saying: *"Favor isn't fair."* God's hand opens doors no strategy can pry open—and no bitterness can block. I tried to help her see this, but she responded with anger, not understanding. Our working relationship became unbearable. Though her tactics were exposed in time, the wounds lingered.

My transition from corporate healthcare to ministry didn't happen overnight. When I first stepped away from the hospital world, I thought I was walking away from one chapter. But God showed me I wasn't leaving—I was being reassigned. Ministry felt like a familiar hospital, but with spiritual patients. The titles were different, but the weight was the same. People still needed healing, leaders still needed development, and toxic behaviors still existed— sometimes even more subtly.

Later, I found myself repeating some of the same missteps I thought I had left behind—responding to conflict by venting instead of praying, or internalizing issues rather than confronting them biblically. I faced situations where my own emotional reactions revealed areas I hadn't yet surrendered to God. I learned that toxic relationships don't just happen around you—they expose what's unresolved within you. Whether it's in a boardroom, a sanctuary, or a living room, unhealthy patterns can show up anywhere. But the earlier we identify them, the sooner we can grow through them.

After serving in ministry for 8 years, I was ordained as a pastor. But even in that sacred process—one that should have felt affirming and holy—I wrestled deeply. Internally, I was still comparing the toxicity I had seen in boardrooms to what I witnessed in ministry. It wasn't just the present pain; it was old pain, too. I had seen the underbelly of church hurt as a child—watched leadership be careless with people, use their platforms to control instead of to cover.

So even as God was elevating me, I battled with distrust. I didn't want a title if it meant I had to turn a blind eye to the same dysfunction. That wrestle was real. But God was patient. He sent my leader—someone I consider a spiritual father—to affirm me, remind me that He called me—not man—and that my healing didn't disqualify me; it prepared me.

He ultimately showed me what the Word says about me: that I am chosen, appointed, and equipped to lead with love, truth, and grace—even when my lens is skewed, and the environment isn't perfect.

Praise is what anchored me.

This chapter isn't just about my experiences; it's about how God used the worst moments to produce the deepest worship—and how He can do the same for you.

As a little girl, I remember Sunday evenings after church, heading to Harold & Belle's with my stepfather, who was in ministry, along with other pastors, bishops, and friends. Sitting at the table, my two pigtails bouncing as I swung my feet—just barely touching the floor—I looked around in awe. To me, I was in the presence of superstars. They drove nice cars, wore sharp suits, and carried themselves with an air of importance. I thought to myself, I can't wait until I get older to do what they do.

When the waitress came over and asked, *"Honey, what would you like to order?"* I heard the pastors around me say, *"You can have anything you want on the menu."* I eagerly pointed to a plate piled high with fried chicken, collard greens, and macaroni and cheese. As I sat there, soaking in the moment, my young mind absorbed more than just the flavors of Southern comfort food—I was also digesting the conversations around me.

I listened as they discussed church drama—who they liked and didn't like, who had what, and what they were doing with the offering money. They compared congregations, measuring success by attendance numbers and material possessions. *"Did you see how many people were at Pastor So-and-So's service today?"* *"Did you see his Rolls Royce?"* *"Is the First Lady wearing St. John's?"* Then there were whispers about the church pianist's sexuality and rumors about who in the choir was involved with whom.

At such a young age, those conversations shaped my perception of relationships and ministry. I equated leadership with status, influence, and competition. But as I grew older, gaining experience in both corporate America and ministry leadership, I came to a sobering realization—toxicity is not limited to boardrooms or business offices. It can thrive in sacred spaces, too.

The truth is ministry should never mirror the world's standards of power, gossip, and comparison. Yet, just like in corporate settings, egos clash, jealousy brews, and people measure success by the wrong metrics. But God never intended for His church to operate like that. True ministry isn't about status—it's about servanthood. It's not about outshining others—it's about out-serving them. And while toxic environments may be common, we are called to be uncommon, choosing integrity over influence, humility over hierarchy, and worship over worldly ambition.

During my time in ministry, I encountered a coworker who often stirred up drama. She thrived on division, manipulating others to gain control in situations. Her behavior created tension among volunteers, and staff turning what should have been a collaborative environment into one full of distrust and conflict. I realized that I had played a role in the tension by responding with frustration and harsh words instead of wisdom. I began to understand that my actions, though defensive in nature, added to the toxic environment rather than improving it.

Recognizing the need to change, I shifted my focus to prayer and praise. I asked God for guidance on how to handle the situation with grace and wisdom. By centering my mind on worship instead of frustration, I experienced peace despite ongoing tension. Eventually, the coworker's behavior was exposed, and leadership addressed the situation directly. Although the process was painful, I learned that worship is a powerful tool in disarming toxic relationships and changing environments.

As a child, I remember my mother warning me never to mix bleach and ammonia. Both had a clear purpose, and both were helpful for cleaning, yet when combined they became toxic. This analogy mirrors relationships. Sometimes, two individuals aren't toxic people—they're just carrying toxic wounds. It's not always about personality clashes or someone being difficult. More often, it's the trauma we've been through, the insecurities we haven't healed, and the emotional baggage we still carry that cause things to erupt. You can have two people with good intentions, but when unhealed pain meets miscommunication or unmet expectations, it creates an unhealthy, explosive dynamic.

That's why emotional maturity matters. You're not just reacting to what's happening—you're reacting to everything that came before it. And if we don't pause long enough to ask, *"Where is this really coming from?"* we'll keep blaming people for wounds they didn't create.

Detoxifying relationships starts with understanding your own patterns first. Because healing doesn't just protect you—it helps you stop bleeding on people who didn't cut you.

Detoxifying relationships

This involves identifying and addressing toxic or unhealthy patterns in your partnership. By recognizing the signs of toxicity and taking proactive steps, you can foster healthier, more fulfilling relationships.

In some cases, walking away may be the healthiest option, but leaving should be done with wisdom and grace. When dealing with toxic relationships or environments, what if we can learn to detoxify the situation. Detoxifying a relationship may require establishing boundaries, adjusting communication methods, or even creating space. Not every relationship needs to be restored, but every exit can still reflect the love of Christ. Walking away in peace rather than bitterness is a powerful testimony of God's presence in your life.

In ministry, toxicity can surface when people chase influence instead of walking in purpose. In corporate settings, it often shows up through competition, control, and self-promotion. These behaviors create environments where tension festers, and trust erodes. That's why detoxifying relationships starts with recognizing that toxicity isn't always about someone being a *"bad person."* More often, it's the result of misunderstandings, unmet expectations, or unresolved wounds that have been left unchecked.

The Bible offers a powerful example in the story of Abraham and Lot. As their households grew, tension arose, and their relationship became strained. Rather than allowing the conflict to fester, Abraham suggested they part ways peacefully. Abraham valued peace over control and trusted God to provide. His decision to step away wasn't rooted in bitterness but in faith. (Genesis 13:8-9)

Just as Abraham walked away to preserve peace, we sometimes must step back to maintain our spiritual and emotional well-being. This isn't an act of defeat but an intentional choice to create room for God's guidance.

Detoxifying toxic relationships involves intentionally cultivating healthy behaviors:

Establish Clear Boundaries – Define expectations in your relationships and communicate those limits with love. Boundaries protect both your mental well-being and the relationship itself.

Confront with Grace – Rather than avoiding conflict or reacting harshly, approach difficult conversations with humility and calmness. Colossians 4:6 reminds us to let our words be *"full of grace, seasoned with salt."* A balanced approach allows truth to be spoken in love.

Release Control – Many toxic environments thrive when one or both individuals grasp for control. Instead of striving to win arguments or manipulate outcomes, trust God to bring clarity and peace. Proverbs 3:5 encourages us to *"trust in the Lord with all our hearts and lean not on our own understanding."*

Respond with Praise – When toxicity surrounds you, turn your focus to worship. Praise invites God's presence and shifts your focus from frustration to gratitude and creates a space for God to work.

Pray for the Other Person – Often, the most powerful change comes when we intercede for those who have hurt us. Prayer doesn't justify their behavior, but it releases you from bitterness and softens your heart toward healing.

Redefine the Win – In corporate settings, success often revolves around personal achievements, climbing the ladder, securing titles, or hitting performance goals. It's a world that rewards hustle, visibility, and results—where your value is often tied to your output. The louder your impact, the greater your recognition.

In ministry, that definition doesn't work. Success isn't about how many people know your name, how full your building is, or how perfectly your event was executed. In the kingdom of God, success is rooted in faithfulness, not flash. It's measured by obedience, not optics. It looks like staying when you'd rather walk out, serving when no one's clapping, and loving people who may never say thank you.

That kind of success isn't always public—and it rarely trends. But it's the type that Jesus modeled. Embracing a servant-leadership mindset means shifting your entire posture. It's about choosing towel over title, and character over clout. The Beatitudes in Matthew 5 outline the heart posture God honors: humility, meekness, mercy, and purity. These aren't qualities that climb ladders—they carry crosses.

So, ask yourself: does your environment reward status, competition, and pride—or does it reflect the fruit of the Spirit? Do you chase validation, or walk in vocation? When you realign with God's definition of success, you detoxify your motives. You stop performing and start ministering. And that shift doesn't just bring peace—it invites God's presence into everything you do.

Identify Your Role in the Dynamic – Just as mixing bleach and ammonia creates a toxic environment; some toxic relationships form when two individuals unknowingly trigger each other's weaknesses. Ask yourself, "Am I contributing to this tension through my own insecurities, pride, or defensiveness?" Self-reflection helps you own your part in the problem and seek God's wisdom for healing.

Embrace Humility as a Weapon Against Toxicity – James 4:6 reminds us that *"God opposes the proud but shows favor to the humble."* Pride escalates conflict, while humility diffuses it. Embracing humility requires choosing vulnerability over defensiveness, which invites God's grace into broken situations.

Jesus modeled these principles throughout His ministry. He confronted the Pharisees directly when their pride threatened to harm others, yet He extended compassion to those seeking repentance. His approach to relationships was marked by grace and strength, never avoiding confrontation but always motivated by love.

These are things I've come to realize:

Gossip comes from insecurity disguised as conversation. Insecure individuals often use gossip as a way to gain attention or validation. By pointing out others' faults, they attempt to conceal their own feelings of inadequacy. The antidote to gossip is building confidence in your God-given identity. When you know who you are in Christ, you won't feel the need to tear others down to elevate yourself.

Competition comes from comparison that breeds discontent. Constantly measuring yourself against others creates a cycle of dissatisfaction. In corporate settings, this may manifest as fighting for promotions or undermining coworkers. In ministry, competition might arise when leaders measure success by attendance numbers or popularity. Focusing on your unique calling eliminates the need to compete. Embrace your role and trust that God has positioned you where you are for a reason.

Jealousy comes from focusing on what you lack instead of what you carry. Jealousy often festers when we focus on what others have rather than appreciating our own gifts and blessings. Developing gratitude shifts our mindset from comparison to contentment.

Praising God While Dealing with Toxic People

Dealing with toxic people can feel overwhelming, but one of the most powerful tools God gives us is praise. Praise invites His presence into situations that seem impossible. When you feel surrounded by negativity, worship helps you shift your focus away from the toxicity and back to God's sovereignty.

The Bible reminds us in Isaiah 61:3 that God will give us *"a garment of praise instead of a spirit of despair."* Praise not only strengthens us internally but also changes the atmosphere around us. When you praise God despite your circumstances, you are declaring that His power is greater than the conflict you are facing.

King Jehoshaphat understood this. In 2 Chronicles 20, when the armies of Ammon, Moab, and Mount Seir surrounded Judah, Jehoshaphat responded with praise. He placed worshippers at the front of his army, singing, *"Give thanks to the Lord, for His love endures forever."* As they praised, God caused confusion in the enemy camp, and their enemies turned on each other. Praise brought victory without a single sword being lifted.

In the same way, when we face toxic situations—whether at work, in ministry, or within our families—praising God can disarm hostility and shift the spiritual atmosphere. Praise invites God to fight on your behalf. It silences the lies of the enemy and strengthens you to respond in love rather than anger.

When I dealt with toxic situations in my career, I often found that praising God softened my own heart. Instead of reacting in frustration, worship reminded me that my identity wasn't defined by the gossip or manipulation I encountered. Praise grounded me in God's truth and gave me the strength to forgive, even when the situation didn't immediately improve.

Praise is not just what we do on Sunday mornings; it is a posture of the heart. It shifts our focus from people and their toxicity to God and His sovereignty. When we are surrounded by toxic behavior's, praise reminds us that our value and purpose come from Him alone. There's a saying until God opens up the next door praise Him in the hallway. I say until God completes what He's doing in the room praise Him in the room. Here are scriptures I meditate on and strategies I use.

PRAISE ALIGNS OUR HEARTS WITH GOD'S PERSPECTIVE

- Toxic environments can cloud our vision and make us feel discouraged, unseen, or undervalued. But when we praise, we declare that God is still in control, even in hostile situations.

- Psalm 34:1 – *"I will bless the Lord at all times; His praise shall continually be in my mouth."*

Strategy: Begin and end your day with intentional praise, focusing on who God is rather than what people are doing around you.

PRAISE KEEPS BITTERNESS FROM TAKING ROOT

- It is easy to let toxicity infect our spirit, but praise acts as a spiritual detox. When we choose to worship instead of complaining, we guard our hearts from resentment.

- Hebrews 12:15 – *"See to it that no one falls short of the grace of God and that no bitter root grows up to cause trouble and defile many."*

Strategy: When facing hostility, replace negative thoughts with gratitude. Keep a praise journal where you write down things you are thankful for, even in difficult situations.

Praise Shifts the Atmosphere

- Toxicity thrives in environments filled with negativity, but praise has the power to shift the atmosphere. Worship invites God's presence into the situation.

- 2 Chronicles 20:22 – *"As they began to sing and praise, the Lord set ambushes against the men who were invading Judah, and they were defeated."*

Strategy: Play worship music in your office, car, or home to set the spiritual tone of your day.

Praise is a Weapon Against the Enemy

- The enemy uses toxic people and situations to discourage us, but praise is an offensive weapon against spiritual attacks.

- Isaiah 61:3 – *"To bestow on them a crown of beauty instead of ashes, the oil of joy instead of mourning, and a garment of praise instead of a spirit of despair."*

Strategy: When faced with conflict or frustration, respond with worship rather than reacting emotionally.

PRAISE REMINDS US OF OUR IDENTITY IN CHRIST

- Toxic environments often make us question our worth, but praise reinforces that we are called, chosen, and secure in Christ—not defined by people's opinions.

- 1 Peter 2:9 – *"But you are a chosen people, a royal priesthood, a holy nation, God's special possession, that you may declare the praises of him who called you out of darkness into his wonderful light."*

Strategy: Speak declarations of truth over yourself daily, affirming who you are in Christ rather than internalizing the words or actions of others.

It's one thing to talk about praise—but how do you actually live it out when you're in the middle of dysfunction? These strategies have helped me stay anchored in God's presence, even when environments felt hostile or people acted out of pain. Here are some practical ways to praise God while navigating toxic relationships:

How to Praise God while dealing with Toxic Relationships

Guard Your Heart & Mind – Philippians 4:8 reminds us to focus on what is true, noble, and praiseworthy. Instead of dwelling on negativity, meditate on God's goodness.

Pray for Those Who Hurt You – Matthew 5:44 teaches us to pray for our enemies. Even when people are hostile, interceding for them shifts our heart posture.

Set Healthy Boundaries – Jesus loved people, but He also withdrew from toxic situations (Mark 1:35). Protect your peace by setting limits on unhealthy conversations.

Keep Your Integrity – Colossians 3:23 reminds us to work as if we are working for the Lord, not for people. No matter the environment, serve with excellence and integrity.

Stay Rooted in the Word – Toxic environments can shake our faith, but Psalm 119:105 tells us that God's Word is a lamp to our feet. Stay anchored in Scripture.

PRACTICAL WAYS TO PRAISE THROUGH TOXICITY

Speak Scripture Aloud: Declaring God's Word over your situation aligns your heart with His promises. Verses like Psalm 34:1, *"I will bless the Lord at all times; His praise shall continually be in my mouth,"* remind you that worship is a lifestyle—not just a response to positive circumstances.

Create a Worship Playlist: Surround yourself with songs that uplift your spirit. Worship music shifts your focus and helps you surrender frustration to God.

Thank God for What He's Already Done: Gratitude breaks the power of negativity. Reflecting on how God has provided for you in the past strengthens your faith in what He's doing now.

Pray While Praising: Turn your worship into a conversation with God. As you praise, invite Him to work in your relationships and circumstances.

Refuse to Engage in Toxic Behavior: Praise refocuses your mind. Instead of returning gossip with gossip, or manipulation with manipulation, pause and worship instead. Praising God quiets your spirit and helps you choose a better response.

During my time writing this chapter, I reflected on toxic relationships from my past. There were some relationships I walked away from, and others where people walked away from me—sometimes without explanation, resolution, or closure. For those moments, I want to say this: I am sorry. But know this—through my praise, I also prayed for you. I prayed that God would bless you, heal you, and give you peace.

Toxic relationships don't always require dramatic confrontation or complete separation. Sometimes, detoxification happens when we shift our behavior, prioritize peace, and entrust God with the outcome.

As Psalm 34:1 reminds us, *"I will bless the Lord at all times; His praise shall continually be in my mouth."* While stepping away may be necessary in some cases, our role is to leave well—releasing bitterness and embracing God's peace in the process.

Every painful encounter presents a choice: to respond with frustration or to respond with praise. I've seen firsthand that choosing praise will shift atmospheres, transform hearts, and invite God to move in ways we cannot imagine.

Praise doesn't eliminate toxic environments overnight, but it empowers you to rise above them. As you reflect on your journey, remember that praise is not only your weapon—it's your witness.

Let your praise become louder than the gossip, stronger than the manipulation, and greater than the pain. When you praise God in the midst of adversity, you testify to His presence, power, and faithfulness in your life.

ABOUT LA CREASE COLEMAN

La Crease Coleman is a wife, mother, proud grandmother, and purpose-driven leader whose life is a living testament to the healing power of faith and the strength found in worship. With over 18 years in ministry and a background as a corporate healthcare executive, La Crease brings a rare and impactful blend of compassion, strategy, and Spirit-led leadership to everything she touches.

As the Local and Global Outreach Pastor, she has led mission teams to more than 69 countries, creating life-changing experiences that bring hope to communities and develop leaders with a heart for service. Whether distributing food to families in need, ministering to those behind prison walls, or walking alongside individuals navigating trauma and identity struggles, La Crease is known for building bridges between brokenness and breakthrough.

Her leadership is deeply rooted in the belief that God meets us in the messy, painful, and often overlooked places of our lives—and that worship is not just a Sunday song, but a lifeline in the trenches of toxic relationships and internal battles.

In her powerful chapter, "Praising God While Dealing with Toxic Relationships," La Crease offers wisdom born from lived experience. She doesn't just write about healing—she's walked it, led others through it, and continues to speak life into those who feel unseen or unheard.

Through this collaboration, her prayer is simple but bold: that readers would rediscover the power of praise, even in the midst of pain—and come away with renewed clarity, courage, and conviction to stand tall, heal deeply, and know that their voice still matters.

Living Out Your Values with Faith-Based Decision-Making

By Desiree Saddler

Are Your Values Aligned with Your Decisions?

The Power of Living by Your Values

Every day, we face a multitude of choices—big and small, from how we treat a stranger to how we approach our careers, relationships, and personal growth. Each decision is a reflection of what we truly value. Yet, many people struggle to align their daily actions with their most deeply held beliefs. The challenge lies not just in identifying our values but in consistently applying them to our decision-making process. In my experience, living out your values, one decision at a time, is the key to leading an authentic and fulfilling life. As believers, we are called to align our lives with God's Word, allowing biblical principles to guide every decision we make.

Proverbs 3:5-6 reminds us: *"Trust in the Lord with all your heart and lean not on your own understanding; in all your ways submit to him, and he will make your paths straight."* This chapter will explore, discover, define and practice your values into a powerful force of integrity and meaning, thus aligning with your faith.

I'm inspired to write about decision-making with faith-based values because it has been my life's work to help organizations and leaders establish and implement value systems.   My company, Saddler Consulting Group Inc., has over 30 years of experience serving the needs of global organizations with an exclusive focus on human resources, executive coaching, organizational development, training, and development needs.

Understanding Your Core Values

Before you can live by your values, you need to understand them clearly. Values are the principles and beliefs that guide our behavior, giving our lives direction and purpose. They help us determine what is truly important, shaping our priorities and influencing our decisions. As Christians, our ultimate source of values should be found in God's Word.

SO, WHAT IS A VALUE?

Values are fundamental beliefs that guide or motivate attitudes, actions, and decisions. They help us determine what is important to us, which in turn helps us make decisions in our lives without regret.

If you aren't sure how to identify what your values are, here are four simple steps to take:

Prayer and Self-Reflection: Take a moment to reflect on times in your life when you felt deeply happy and fulfilled. When were you most proud? What was happening? What qualities or principles were at play? Seek God's wisdom in understanding the values He wants you to embody. James 1:5 says, *"If any of you lacks wisdom, you should ask God, who gives generously to all without finding fault, and it will be given to you."*

Examine Your Role Models and Biblical Role Models: Consider the individuals you admire most. What characteristics and qualities do they embody that resonate with you? Start incorporating them into your life. Christ is our perfect example of how to live. Study His life and teachings to determine which values are essential. 1 John 2:6

states, *"Whoever claims to live in Him must live as Jesus did."* Consider figures like Joseph, Daniel, Esther, and Paul, who remained steadfast in their values despite facing challenges.

Look at Past Decisions: Consider major choices you've made—both good and bad. What values were influencing those decisions? What lessons did or can you learn from your past decisions?

Create a List Based on Your Heart's Convictions: Write down a list of values that are important to you. Then, narrow it down to your top three to five core values. These should be the guiding principles that define who you are and how you want to live. What biblical principles resonate deeply with you? Is it honesty, love, humility, or justice?

Through my practice, we provide real-world context to organizations and leaders that we serve by using the VALUES acronym as a way to remind our clients what values should stand for:

V = vital
A= abundant
L= loving
U= understanding
E= edifying
S= satisfying

Let's Take a Deeper Dive into Living and Thriving with a Faith-Based Value System

In the following sections, I'll share three stories and faith-based solutions, providing a biblical framework drawn from personal case studies from my own life experiences.

Story #1: *"Be Willing to Stay, Ready to Leave"*

The first story I would like to share involves leaving a lucrative corporate career to start my business. Once my job became misaligned with my values (i.e., family), it was a decision that wasn't as scary as the unknown.

Earlier in my career, I was well-respected as a Human Resources Director. However, after returning from maternity leave, my work world crumbled because my new supervisor proved to be a very challenging manager. I recall being miserable reporting to this person despite my numerous attempts to work with him effectively. It's unclear what his motivation was, but it felt like he was actively trying to ruin my reputation with his abusive and self-serving behavior.

As a leadership advisor and coach, I tried to persevere and push through this challenging situation by applying the many tools and techniques I had taught hundreds of managers every day to use during difficult times. However, there came a point where it started negatively affecting my health. I knew something had to change because I felt like I was bringing my whole family down when I came home. I was exhausted and curt with my husband and children.

As a person who is strong in her faith-based convictions and core values, I let my trusted network of people know that I was struggling in my professional life. They could see that showing up to work was gut-wrenching for me daily, negatively affecting my physical, mental, and spiritual well-being. Something had to change, but I needed a plan and a strategy in place before I made my move.

How did I garner the courage and confidence to leave a stable, excellent reputation and well-paying job? Why would I take a risk that could be financially detrimental to my family? Read on to see how I reframed the risk into a blossoming career opportunity.

I decided to confide in my trusted friend, who shares my faith and values. As providence would have it, she is now my senior consultant at my company. We brainstormed different ways to address my toxic work situation, and she remarked that I'd always wanted to start my own business, *"Why not now, Desiree? What's stopping you?"* With 15 years of Human Resources experience, I have come to understand the truth in the adage, *"People don't leave companies; they leave bad managers."* So, I began putting together a plan to exit the corporate world, allowing me not only to escape a bad manager and a miserable situation but also to pursue a long-term goal of mine. While developing my exit strategy, I remained 100% present in my current position, demonstrating my value and contributions at work (Willing to Stay), all while dedicating a few hours a week to working on my business plan (Ready to Leave).

I utilized a Gap Analysis decision-making tool to help me identify the steps necessary to launch my business. After discussing with my husband, I then chose a few more trusted colleagues and prayer warriors in my life to confide in and spiritually support me during the transition. Within six months, I was able to open my doors and start taking clients. That was the beginning of starting my business, and in 2026, I will be celebrating 20 happy and prosperous years of working for myself, as well as providing work opportunities for many independent contractors.

When making decisions, the lesson learned was to be *"willing to stay, ready to leave"*. Being willing to stay means being willing to show your worth and show them how you shine in your profession. Maintain your high work ethic and give it your all. Be the best that you can be at the moment. Being ready to go means always having your resume updated and consistently maintaining a networking mindset to share your goals, dreams, and aspirations with others. Always ask for prayer for guidance before making a decision. When you are willing to stay and ready to leave, it empowers you to know that God is in control of the outcome of your decision, regardless of where you ultimately end up.

If you want to do your own Gap Analysis – Here are some simple steps:

Step 1: List the current state you are experiencing at the moment.

Step 2: List and imagine it is 6 months or a year from now, and you've accomplished this goal or made the decision you need to make. Imagine you are at a future moment, looking back on how things unfolded.

Step 3: Then fill in the Gap by answering questions like: What happened? What went well? What could be some challenges? What were the steps you had to take? How would it feel? Taste? Smell? Look? Sound? How did you grow? What would your celebration look like?

Story #2: *"There is no such thing as a bad decision…as long as you have done your due diligence. Your decision will be made with NO REGRETS!"*

    This second story reveals how core values guide your actions. Six years into opening my consulting firm, I began a 3-month project to work with a large entertainment company in their human resources department, redesigning their performance management process. This was a perfect opportunity, as I worked only 20-30 hours a week, according to my schedule. So, it allowed me to be a present wife, the mother I wanted to be for my young sons and also to continue to grow my business. The 3-month assignment extended to 6 months, as I served as an interim in their now-vacant VP of HR position until they found a permanent replacement.

I worked so well with the Leadership Team and CFO that the 6 months turned into another 2 years! We also found it challenging to fill the permanent VP of HR position. One day, the CFO surprised me and offered me the permanent VP of HR position. She was very complimentary: *"You understand our team. We like working with you, so why don't you just take the position?"* My first thought was, *"WOW! When I worked in various corporations, I never advanced to the VP position. This was an amazing opportunity!"* She said, *"Take your time, talk it over with your husband, and then give me an answer next week."*

My husband and I prayed about the opportunity, weighed the pros and cons, considered how our financial situation would benefit from the significant increase, and even thought about the fringe benefits. However, at the time, my oldest son had several medical issues, one of which was a pending brain surgery at 8 years old. I needed to have a flexible schedule that allowed me to take him back and forth to Children's Hospital.

That weekend, my husband and I devised a decision-making activity to provide us with clarity and confidence. We came up with a list of things to consider if I were to take the position that we (1) can't have, (2) must have, and (3) would be nice to have in our lives.

After analyzing our research and considering all aspects of the situation, we decided it was best for our family if I didn't take the position. People often ask me if I regret not taking advantage of such a lucrative opportunity. I said *"no"* because we had considered all aspects and prayed about the decision, and I have no regrets to this day.

The critical lesson learned is there is no such thing as a bad decision if you have done the research and gathered all the information provided at the time you made the decision. Values and faith-based decision-making allow you to make faster and more confident decisions without regrets. When making a decision, list the things that you (1) can't have, (2) must have, and (3) would be nice to have in your life.

Story #3: Finding Balance in Your Decisions and Values: Not All Money is Good Money

This third story focuses on how your decisions and values are aligned. What if you are struggling to balance financial considerations and personal values when making important life decisions? At this point in my career, I had been running my business for over a decade and had a significant contract with a mid-sized non-profit company. I was providing Sexual Harassment Prevention training for all of their leaders, which is required by the state. I also was coaching their HR Manager on employee-related issues. I was horrified to discover that the CEO had been overly friendly with several female employees, particularly his secretary.

I had no hesitation in approaching him about it. I counseled him to stop immediately, as the hostile work environment it could create, the impact on declining morale within the organization, and the potential destruction of his reputation were all significant concerns. The in-house HR Manager confirmed my observations by sharing complaints that had been reported by female employees and other employees witnessing the CEO's behavior.

I insisted that he attend my sexual harassment class so he would finally understand that his questionable behavior was not welcome and very much illegal. His bold behavior escalated to the point where other executives witnessed him flirting with his secretary during class. I promptly documented the incident and placed him on a performance improvement plan, which he failed to meet. At this point, I knew I couldn't continue working with him and his blatant disregard for my repeated counsel to stop his behavior.

I informed him immediately that I could no longer, in good conscience, continue consulting on this project and that I would terminate our contract immediately. In anger, he questioned me and said, *"You are just going to walk away from this good money?"* And I replied confidently, *"Yes!"*

That's where the concept of *"not all money is good money"* applies as the lesson learned. Did you earn it cleanly and ethically?

Because I had been making decisions based on my values for years, it was an easy and quick decision, with no regrets. Walk away with your head held high, knowing you stood by your values and principles rather than prioritizing financial gain. Aligning Your Decisions with Your Faith-Based Values ensures that your actions consistently reflect them. This requires conscious effort, self-awareness, and a heart attuned to God's guidance.

How to Make Value-Based Decisions

Pause, Reflect, and Seek God's Guidance through Prayer: Before making a decision, take a moment to ask yourself, *"Does this align with my values?" "Does this align with God's will?"* Philippians 4:6 reminds us, *"Do not be anxious about anything, but in every situation, by prayer and petition, with thanksgiving, present your requests to God."* If a choice contradicts your principles, reconsider your approach.

Set Intentions: Each day, remind yourself of your values and make a conscious effort to apply them in your decisions.

Use a Biblical Decision-Making Framework: When facing a difficult choice, list your values and analyze which option best aligns with them. If a decision supports integrity, honesty, compassion, love, and obedience to God, it's likely the right one.

Seek External Accountability by Seeking Godly Counsel: Share your values with trusted friends, mentors, colleagues, fellow Christians, and ministers who can help keep you accountable and offer wisdom. Proverbs 11:14 says, *"For lack of guidance a nation falls, but victory is won through many advisers. "*.

Embrace Consistency, Trust, and Obey: Even when it's hard, obeying God leads to blessings. Luke 11:28 states, *"Blessed are those who hear the word of God and obey it."* Living out your values isn't about grand gestures—it's about consistent, small decisions that reinforce your beliefs over time. These are decisions that you can live with and take pride in.

OVERCOMING CHALLENGES TO LIVING YOUR VALUES

Living by your values isn't always easy. Sometimes, external pressures, fear, or convenience tempt you to compromise. Recognizing these obstacles and preparing strategies to navigate them is essential. Read on to learn how social pressure, fear of judgment, difficult trade-offs, self-doubt, and temptation for convenience are all common challenges we have to overcome as faith-based decision-makers.

Social pressure can sometimes lead friends, family, or society to push you to act against your values. Stay firm by reminding yourself why your values matter, and practice assertive communication to maintain your stance. The world may push you to act against your values. Romans 12:2 advises, *"Do not conform to the pattern of this world, but be transformed by the renewing of your mind."*

Fear of judgment leads to worry about how others perceive you. Remember that authenticity often inspires respect, and those who genuinely support you will appreciate your integrity. Jesus said in Matthew 5:16, *"Let your light shine before others, that they may see your good deeds and glorify your Father in heaven."*

Sometimes, living by your values requires making **tough sacrifices.** Consider the long-term benefits of staying true to yourself rather than seeking short-term comfort. Jesus reminds us in Mark 8:36, *"What good is it for someone to gain the whole world, yet forfeit their soul?"*

Self-doubt comes when you second-guess yourself. Keep a journal to remind you how living out your values has positively impacted your life. Talk with others to remind yourself what your purpose is and what truly makes you happy.

The temptation for convenience is a difficult one for many people: Taking shortcuts, procrastination, or compromising your values may seem more straightforward, but in the long run, it leads to dissatisfaction. Practice patience and resilience. 1 Corinthians 10:13 reassures us, *"No temptation has overtaken you except what is common to mankind. And God is faithful; he will not let you be tempted beyond what you can bear."*

Living Your Values in Different Areas of Your Life

Your values should be evident in every aspect of your life. Here's how you can incorporate them into the key areas of personal growth, relationships, career and work ethic, community and social responsibility, and health and well-being.

Commit to personal growth in your life: Commit to continuous self-improvement in alignment with your values. Select educational opportunities, books, and courses that align with your core values and beliefs. Practice self-discipline and mindfulness to stay connected with your values. Choose activities and habits that reflect godly principles. Colossians 3:23 says, *"Whatever you do, work at it with all your heart, as working for the Lord."*

Communicate openly and honestly: In your relationships, even when it's complicated.

Set boundaries to protect your values and emotional well-being. Don't be afraid to teach and share with people the best way to treat or speak to you. Surround yourself with people who respect and uphold your principles and can serve as a sounding board. Love others unconditionally, just as Christ loves us. John 13:34 commands, *"Love one another. As I have loved you, so you must love one another."* Be honest and kind, even in the midst of conflict. Ephesians 4:15 tells us to *"speak the truth in love."*

Career and work ethic will dictate the life you lead: Choose a career path that aligns with your values rather than just financial gain. Proverbs 16:11 states, *"Honest scales and balances belong to the Lord; all the weights in the bag are of his making."* Lead with integrity, honesty, and a commitment to excellence. Mark 10:45 reminds us, *"For even the Son of Man did not come to be served, but to serve."* Advocate for ethical practices and positive workplace culture.

Be an active member of your community and take on social responsibility: Contribute to causes that resonate with your values through volunteering, donations, or advocacy. Be a responsible citizen by making informed decisions and treating others with kindness, respect, and fairness in your daily interactions. Be generous and compassionate. Proverbs 19:17 states, *"Whoever is kind to the poor lends to the Lord, and he will reward them."* Stand for justice. Micah 6:8 declares, *"To act justly and to love kindly and to walk humbly with your God."*

Make your health and well-being a priority: Your lifestyle choices reflect self-respect and care for your body. Honor your body as God's temple. 1 Corinthians 6:19-20 says, *"Do you not know that your bodies are temples of the Holy Spirit?"* Maintain mental and emotional balance through mindfulness, gratitude, and stress management. Philippians 4:7 promises, *"The peace of God, which transcends all understanding, will guard your hearts and your minds in Christ Jesus."* Seek medical and psychological support when needed without compromising your values. Don't worry about what others may think or say.

THE RIPPLE EFFECT OF LIVING OUT YOUR FAITH-BASED VALUES

When you consistently live by your values, you transform your life and inspire others to do the same. Authenticity breeds trust and respect, creating a ripple effect that encourages those around you to act with integrity. The benefits of living by your values are numerous: Knowing that your actions align with your beliefs brings a sense of fulfillment and inner peace. Your relationships will become stronger. Honesty and integrity foster deeper, more meaningful connections. You will have increased confidence–Making value-based decisions reinforces self-trust and confidence.

Get comfortable in your S.K.I.N*. This acronym stands for:
Self-esteem building
Knowing yourself (the good and the bad)
Intuition is your friend (God gave it to you, so use it), and last of all

Negating that Negative Self-Talk (Use positive affirmations).

Your actions can inspire others to live authentically and make ethical choices. Feel good about who you are despite any flaws you may have. Stop comparing yourself to others and be content with who you are, and the gifts God has given you. Work on those gifts and use those gifts to feel confident about the decisions you have to make in your life without regrets.

Conclusion: Making Each Decision Count

Living out your values one decision at a time requires intentionality, but the rewards are immense. Every choice is an opportunity to glorify God and reinforce who you are and what you stand for. Colossians 3:17 sums it up: *"And whatever you do, whether in word or deed, do it all in the name of the Lord Jesus, giving thanks to God the Father through him."*

Remember, your values are not just abstract ideals—they are the foundation for the life you create.

Stay true to your faith and values, and you will shape a life of purpose and integrity, establishing a fulfilling and meaningful path forward, one decision at a time, with no regrets.

Follow-up questions for you to consider

- What specific values do you and your family prioritize in your decision-making process?

- What lessons did you learn from the shared stories about values and decision-making approaches?

- How have your value-based decisions impacted you throughout your career and personal life?

- How can you balance financial considerations with your values when making important life decisions?

- What stood out to you in this chapter about aligning your values with your decisions?

- What tips and lessons did you learn about the importance of living without regrets?

ABOUT DESIREE SADDLER

Desiree Saddler is a powerhouse in people development and a champion for strong, thriving teams.

As the Principal and Owner of Saddler Consulting Group, she brings over 25 years of experience helping organizations around the world—from Fortune 500 companies to mission-driven nonprofits—unlock their full potential through human-centered leadership and organizational strategy.

With a deep passion for communication, emotional intelligence, and workplace culture, Desiree has delivered more than 10,000 workshops and built powerful learning experiences that equip leaders to connect, communicate, and lead with clarity. Her work spans a range of industries including banking, entertainment, manufacturing, and beyond—all grounded in her belief that great teams are built on trust, understanding, and purpose.

Armed with a Master's in Organization Management and a B.A. in Psychology with an emphasis in HR, Desiree is certified in 13 top-tier behavioral and leadership tools, including MBTI, DISC, and Situational Leadership II. She also serves as Faculty for the American

Management Association and a Franklin Covey Training Delivery Consultant—roles that reflect both her expertise and her commitment to lasting transformation.

Known for her strategic mind and servant heart, Desiree partners with clients not just to meet their development goals—but to exceed them. Her work is guided by faith, rooted in purpose, and driven by a calling to empower people to lead with integrity, empathy, and impact.

I Forgive You, But I Still Have Trauma

By Torrian Scott

If you're going to live, understand that there is a stark possibility that you will be hurt. Jesus said it best in John 16:33 AMPC, *"In the world you have tribulation and trials and distress and frustration."* No truer words can be spoken of this human experience. But what He says at the end is shocking, *"But be of good cheer, for I have overcome the world."* In a world and a life full of hurt, how could a person *"be of good cheer?"* How could they have an overcoming mindset, when life has dealt a brutal blow?

What I hope to help you gain through this chapter is solace in knowing that the problems you face are not proprietary to you.

Also, I hope to help you develop the confidence you need in order to experience the overcoming power of forgiveness in life, love, and leadership.

If you are reading this, there is a good chance that you are a leader in some capacity in your line of work, your business, or in the community. Not only are you a leader, but you are also a high performing leader who has their heart set on operating at the apex of your purpose and potential in order to make an impact in the sphere of your expertise. If this is true for you – you are what I call a *"Master in the Marketplace."* As a Master in the Marketplace, your propensity to feel and be impacted by distress and frustration is no different from any other who is living on this earth.

Our workplaces, organizations, businesses, and society is filled with issues and people with problems. Big Problems. Sometimes those problems are low impact, and other times we can find ourselves in the midst of cataclysmic problems that threaten our progress and impact in leadership, and sometimes our very existence.

In life and leadership, conflicts arise, betrayals sting, and discouragement sets in. Whether you're an entrepreneur, a corporate leader, or an industry disruptor, one thing remains constant: people will disappoint you - not just once, but multiple times; causing a level of mistrust and callousness that could lead to PTSD.

We are called to a higher standard—one that reflects the nature of the King and the Kingdom in all our dealings. When distress and frustration arise in our lives and leadership; what matters most is what we do with that disappointment, how we create space for mistakes, and how we bounce back stronger in that area after a setback. As a Master in the Marketplace, you and I do not have the luxury of adopting a *"dog-eat-dog"* style of leadership, where we hold onto grudges and use it as fuel for advancement or to make a point to those who have wronged us.

In my years of executive coaching high performing leaders in both the public and private sector, I've helped them navigate the difficulty of *"people problems"*. I've been invited into offices, boardrooms, and the sacred spaces of their lives to hear about corporate betrayal, colleague misconduct, employee insubordination, and industry failures in hopes to find the solution that helps them overcome the difficulty.

Have you ever heard the quote, *"how you do anything, is how you do everything?"* Well, through all of the problems, distresses, and frustrations I've heard, counseled, and coached leaders through – I've noticed a trend and have come to the conclusion that; How a leader processes and remedies the problems that they face in public, directly correlates to the way they have handled these issues in the private areas of their lives. Avoidance, aggression, cold shoulders, disengagement, and retaliation can all be seen in the way leaders handle their problems in public and in private. There is a better way to deal, so let's talk about it because trauma and PTSD can be from anyone, but it affects us most when it is from people we love.

Family Is God's Design

Family was God's original blueprint for community, love, and purpose. God creates a perfect environment where everything could grow in complete harmony with one another. No one thing benefiting more from another, simply paradise. As soon as Adam and Eve start their partnership together, outside forces begin to disrupt that partnership and threaten humanity's euphoric unrestrained relationship with their Creator and each other. From the very beginning, the enemy has sought to destroy this union between God and Man, and Man and Woman, And Between Parents and Children. Why? Because unity within the family reflects God's Divine order, and division is the enemy's most effective weapon against that order.

Not to make this a Bible Study, but consider the very first breakdowns in community, trust, fidelity, and confidence - The Family. Want to talk about **Bitterness and self-preservation**? Look no further than Adam and Eve. Want to talk about jealousy, slander, and murder -- look no further than Cain & Able. What about guilt, shame, and hiding secrets, have you heard about Tamar? Malice and hatred?

Take a look at David & Absolom's story. The list could go on how these leaders suffered greatly in their leadership roles because of unresolved issues at home. You see, the enemy does not begin his attack on your boardroom, workplace, or gym buddies—he starts with the foundation - the family. If he can disrupt unity at home, he can fracture communities, derail destinies, and even weaken your effectiveness in your place of purpose.

"Offense is no coincidence; it's a strategy. The enemy despises unity, while God despises division."

Proverbs 6:16-19 reminds us that among the things the Lord hates, one of them is *"he who sows discord among brethren."* The enemy seeks to entangle us in bitterness, unforgiveness, and self-righteousness, so we fail to recognize the chains he's placed on our hearts. Those chains become a trait of our character as a result of our habits, and Warren Buffet said it best, *"habits are like chains, too loose to notice, until they are too tight to break."*

1 John 4:20-21 challenges us: *"If someone says, 'I love God,' and hates his brother, he is a liar."* The real test of our love for God is how we treat those who have wronged us. So these next few pages are designed to help navigate you through and recover from some of the most devastating blows you can take as a leader - in the area of your family.

Family Feud: I forgive you, but I still have trauma!

Forgiveness is often taught as a moment—a single decision. But what happens when you've forgiven, yet the wounds remain? If you're like me, then you've experienced some of these thoughts:

- I forgive you, but the pain lingers.

- I forgive you, but I still feel rejected.

- I forgive you, but anxiety rises when I hear your name.

- I forgive you, but I'm unsure if I can trust you again.

- I forgive you, but I still have trauma.

Many of us have been deeply hurt—betrayed, let down, or disregarded. This is a common human experience. Paul writes to the Corinthian church, that *"there is no temptation that has taken you except that which is common to man."* One of the first things that the enemy loves to do is to pressure a person into isolation and attack with bitterness and resentment. Like a young gazelle removed from the herd; weak, vulnerable, and without protection becomes the prime target for a predator, so does a person who isolates in the caves of bitterness.

Most people have the mindset that they are the only one struggling through the process of forgiveness, dealing with the stressors of leadership, and feeling helpless as the trauma of past errors and mistakes makes it hard to move forward in confidence. So we build walls of self-preservation, thinking we are protecting our hearts when, in reality, we are imprisoning our hearts.

The Heart-Set: Guarding vs. Hardening

Your heart functions like a thermostat—it sets the temperature of all your relationships. If your heart is set on disappointment, anger, or mistrust, every interaction with that person will trigger those emotions.

One leader once told me, *"No one can make me go from calm to rage like my family."* That's because the thermostat of their heart was set on disappointment. They were stuck in a disappointment gap—this happens when their experience doesn't meet their expectation, frustrated by what their loved one should have been but never became, how they should behave but didn't. This gap causes disappointment, disenchantment, bitterness, and hardness of heart to set in making it very hard for a person to fully forgive that person.

Proverbs 18:19 AMP reads *"A brother offended is harder to win over than a fortified city, and contentions [separating families] are like the bars of a castle."*

LEADERSHIP FRAMEWORK: Bridging the Gap Between Expectation and Experience

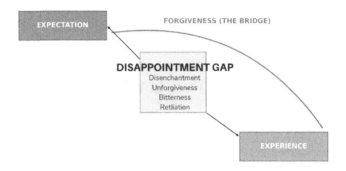

The only way to bridge the gap is not lowering your expectations, but arriving at peace through intentional, heartfelt, and continuous forgiveness.

Guard Your Heart, But Don't Harden It

The Bible tells us to guard our hearts (Proverbs 4:23) because it determines the course of our lives. What I've found is that what most people call *"guarding"* their hearts is actually more along the lines of *"hardening"* their heart.

If we think in terms of gardening; a smart farmer will put a protective fence around their garden to keep out pest and predators that threatened the productivity of the garden. If that farmer decides to build a thick wall around the perimeter of the garden and enclose it with an iron roof, he not only will keep out the predators and pests, but also smother the potential of life in the garden.

A hardened heart is much like that. It is a stone and iron fortress— locked up, inaccessible, and void of life. Some of us have placed our hearts in maximum security, allowing no one access—not even God. This is a hard place to live, because it isolates you and I from the most powerful purpose in our lives – community.

I once had a client who was overcoming a verbal and physically abusive marriage. As we coached further, it was apparent that she had hardened her heart against the possibility of ever being able to operate freely in her love life. This greatly impaired her ability to lead in her consulting practice. To make matters worse, she also had a level of survivor's guilt. Shortly after she mustered up enough courage to leave him, he was involved in a fatal car accident. After a few sessions of tackling this problem, we finally got to the root of the problem; she was mad at God for not warning her against her abuser and rescuing her from this difficult situation. Not only that, but she also blamed herself for not being "good enough" for him and found it hard to forgive herself.

Through a forgiveness framework I developed, she came to realize that healing required her to close the disappointment gap and release the hardness in her heart—toward her late husband, toward herself, and even toward God. Ultimately, she had to embrace the truth that real healing could only come **from trusting**

the God in Heaven who could restore her heart, rather than clinging to the pain caused by the one on Earth who broke it.

As *"Masters in The Marketplace"*, we must learn to lead and live with a bleeding heart—one that remains tender and responsive, even after pain.

This is a tough road to travel, but understand, once you make the decision to travel down it, you will find yourself very shortly at the beautiful destination called *"forgiveness"*.

Taking the First Step to Forgiveness

Many of us wait for the other person to apologize before we consider reconciliation. But what if God is calling you to take the first step?

Understand this, *"An apology is never a prerequisite for forgiveness. Forgiveness is more about confronting what's in you, rather than confronting others."*

I remember a time when I was treated unfairly by a former boss. I felt completely justified in my stance against their behavior. Yet, one day, the Holy Spirit prompted me to write a letter asking for forgiveness. I was taken aback—*"why should I apologize when I had done no wrong?"*

In that moment, I realized the real issue: the condition of my heart. I had become prideful and self-justified. However, Scripture convicted me: *"So if you are presenting a sacrifice at the altar in the Temple and you suddenly remember that someone has something against you, 24 leave your sacrifice there at the altar. Go and be reconciled to that person. Then come and offer your sacrifice to God."* – Matthew 5:23

Obeying God in the area of forgiveness is not just about the other person—it's about freedom for yourself. When we take that first step, it opens the door for healing, restoration, and deliverance from the harmful effects of unforgiveness.

The Harmful Realities of Unforgiveness

Unforgiveness is more than just a spiritual burden—it has tangible, physical consequences. Studies show that unresolved bitterness can lead to increased stress, high blood pressure, and even chronic illness. Some cases of cancer and other debilitating diseases have been linked to long-standing resentment with a close family member.

I once heard a heartbreaking story of a woman who suffered from a serious illness. After exhausting every medical option, she was encouraged to explore whether unforgiveness was playing a role in her condition. Through deep reflection and prayer, she recalled years of unresolved pain with her father. When she finally chose to forgive—her health dramatically improved. Her body had been holding onto the poison of bitterness, and once she released it, healing followed.

Psalm 139:23-24 gives us a powerful invitation: *"Search me, O God, and know my heart; test me and know my anxious thoughts. See if there is any offensive way in me, and lead me in the way everlasting."*

Let this be a moment of self-examination. Ask the Holy Spirit to reveal any hidden places of unforgiveness in your heart whether they stem from your childhood, private life, or public professional life. True freedom comes when we surrender completely to His process of healing.

MASTERING FORGIVENESS: A SIGN OF MATURITY

Forgiveness is not weakness; it is mastery. It's a mastery over the temptations to throw people away, put every person at bay in fears of them hurting you, and ultimately harden your heart and cut off the effectiveness you can obtain as a leader in the marketplace. As we grow, certain things should no longer shake us the way they used to.

How you respond to certain conflicts should improve and your recovery time should shorten as you gain forgiveness mastery.

This type of mastery, like any place of mastery, will take intention, discipline, and patience as you navigate the recesses of your heart. To do that two things are necessary. 1). Come to the conclusion that God's method has always been reconciliation, just look at Matthew 18:35, John 3:16, and 2 Peter 3:9. There is no way around it. He made us for each other. There are some places where *"trust and reconciliation"* are not possible due to the time lapse or the nature of the offense. Maybe that person died, is incapacitated, doesn't know that they've offended you - or better yet, doesn't even care that they've offended you. Still, forgiveness is a personal responsibility that we accept regardless of an apology. As believers we are called to live at peace. I remember reading Romans 12:17-19 for the first time, and I was appalled that as things are done to us, that we are to make a decision to live at peace with all men.

"Repay no one evil for evil. Have regard for good things in the sight of all men. If it is possible, as much as depends on you, live peaceably with all men. Beloved, do not avenge yourselves, but rather give place to wrath; for it is written, "Vengeance is Mine, I will repay," says the Lord." – Romans 12:17-19.

Paul shares that we as believers, should take responsibility for the condition of our heart, and God will take care of the rest!

WHO SHALL I FORGIVE?

I have found that forgiveness extends to three key areas: forgiving others, forgiving organizations, and forgiving ourselves. Unforgiveness in any of these areas can have adverse effects on our health, our ability to reason, our leadership, and ultimately our destiny. Jesus warns us the dangers of failing to forgive in Matthew 19:21-35, *"So also My heavenly Father will do to you if you do not forgive— each one his brother— from your hearts."*

THE THREE STEP FRAMEWORK TO FORGIVENESS:

Forgiving others, organizations, and ourselves takes the same three steps:

1. Forgiveness by Faith
2. The Heart Cleanse
3. Limitless Forgiveness

In my book, Running After Destiny, I detail these areas extensively, but here is an overview:

1. Forgiveness by Faith - Forgiveness, like love, is not a feeling—it is a decision. A decision to keep no record of wrongdoing, as 1 Corinthians 10:4-8 details. It is choosing to relinquish the desire to see someone suffer for what they've done—their negligence, their egregious behaviors, and their intentional or unintentional offense. This decision is difficult to sustain, which is why we need principle #2: The Heart Cleanse.

2. The Heart Cleanse - This step involves taking the decision to forgive and bathing it in prayer. Often, the enemy of our soul—Satan—will attempt to stir up anger, resentment, and bitterness, reminding us of past offenses. However, we must take a page from Jesus' book by looking at His example on the cross.

There He was, suspended between heaven and earth, flesh torn, spinal cord exposed, beaten beyond recognition, nailed at agonizing angles. To breathe, He had to push up on His nailed feet to gasp for air. Betrayed and denied by one of His own, forsaken by all, at the height of His suffering—He found the strength and courage to pray these words: ***"Father, forgive them, for they know not what they do."***

Jesus demonstrated that He practiced what He preached. He told the disciples, *"Pray for those who despitefully use you."* On the cross, He prayed for His betrayers, deniers, mockers, forsakers, and all those who did not believe in Him. How much more should we forgive those who simply *"do not know what they are doing"* when they hurt us?

3. Limitless Forgiveness - This principle is personal to me. My biological father was not consistently present in my life, but one year, we finally got the chance to talk. By then, I was 27—graduated from college, married the woman of my dreams, had a one-year-old, lived in a dream home in Houston, worked a great job, and drove my dream car. He had missed a lot.

However, on March 31, 2011 on a random phone call, he told me something I had never heard him say before: **"Son, I love you—I never wanted you to think I didn't love you."**

Those words pierced my heart, swallowing years of uncertainty, fear, anger, and insecurity. We exchanged texts and calls for months. In August of that same year, I received a harrowing Facebook message from my cousin: My father had been shot—murdered—by his own stepson.

I was devastated. Rage, retaliation, and anxiety filled my heart. After weeks of grieving and praying, God interrupted me with a series of questions:

God: *Son, are you forgiven?*

Me: *(Trembling) Yes.*

God: *So, when your time is up, you'll be with Me in Heaven, yes?*

Me: *Yes.*

God: *If that young man asks for forgiveness, will I forgive him?*

Me: *(Reluctantly) Yes.*

God: *And when his time on Earth is up, will he not be with Me in Heaven as well?*

Me: *(More reluctant) Yes.*

God: *Haven't you been taught that the realities of Heaven can be experienced on Earth? "Your Kingdom come, Your will be done on earth as it is in Heaven."*

Me: *Yes.*

God: *So, riddle Me this: You're hanging out with Moses, David, and Samson. Then, this young man who killed your father strolls down the streets of gold. Do you think, in that moment, you will recall what he did and go to war against him with Moses's Staff, David's Stone and Sling, or Samson's Jawbone?*

Me: *(Somber yet understanding) No, sir.*

God: *True forgiveness, son, is treating a person on Earth the way you would treat them in Heaven. That is true forgiveness.*

From that day on, I got the message, and I hope you do as well. No matter if someone offends you, if that offense leads to an organization's failure, or if you struggle to forgive yourself—walk in limitless forgiveness. You don't have to walk around with the trauma.

I leave you with this scripture that helped me overcome the pain, trauma, guilt, shame, and overwhelming unforgiveness I had in my heart for others, organizations, and myself. It is found in **Hebrews 9:14**—*"How much more will the blood of Christ, who through the eternal Spirit offered Himself unblemished to God, cleanse our consciences from dead works so that we may serve the living God?"*

This scripture painted the beauty of forgiveness and its realities on my heart. I didn't have to be bound by the past traumas, I could be free as God takes the sacrifice of Jesus and applies it to my consciousness - the seat of my belief system- and does a deep cleaning so that I can recall certain grievances, but without the pain. My heart has been cleansed and washed to receive the healing God promises.

He gives us the ability to forgive like He does us.

A CALL TO ACTION

Forgiveness is not about excusing the offense—it's about freeing yourself from its grip. Who do you need to forgive today? What grudge have you carried for too long? You have a choice: to stay bound by the chains of bitterness or to release them and walk in freedom.

I challenge you—yes, you—to take a moment right now. Ask yourself: Who shall I forgive? Write their names down. Pray over them. Release them into the hands of God. As you do this you will experience the peace that surpasses all understanding and knowledge

Because when you forgive, you are most like Christ. And when you walk in limitless forgiveness, you walk in limitless freedom that He provides.

Healing Beyond Words

True healing in families often requires more than just words—it requires consistent action. Trust is rebuilt through patterns of love, through small daily decisions to show up differently than before. For some, this means setting new boundaries. For others, it means extending an invitation to talk. And for all of us, it means keeping our hearts open to God's guidance on how to restore what was broken.

The enemy has long worked to divide families, business partners and colleagues, but God is calling his people to be countercultural – to fight for love, unity and restoration.

Let this chapter be a catalyst where healing begins in you and your world. Let this be the moment where chains of generational pain are broken. Let this be the time where we choose love over resentment, reconciliation over revenge, and freedom over bitterness. Let us walk in limitless forgiveness towards others, organizations, and ourselves. As we practice this, we will begin to experience the peace of God, the Grace to be of "good cheer" in the midst of difficulties, and stand secure knowing that we have forgiven beyond the trauma!

ABOUT TORRIAN SCOTT

Torrian Scott is a transformational voice in faith-driven leadership, blending bold vision with practical wisdom to equip leaders for lasting impact. As the Founder of Mastery Advisory Group and an award-winning business and leadership advisor,  Torrian has spent over 25 years guiding individuals, teams, and organizations to gain clarity of purpose, execute with precision, and lead with legacy in mind.

From Fortune 500 CEOs to professional sports coaches, entrepreneurs, and government leaders, Torrian's influence spans sectors and industries—yet his message remains consistent: greatness starts with alignment, faith, and focus.

A captivating executive coach, conference speaker, and author, Torrian brings truth with fire—engaging audiences in settings ranging from intimate leadership circles to packed arenas. Whether through one-on-one coaching, small group facilitation, or dynamic stage presence, he delivers insight that resonates and transformation that lasts.

Beyond the boardroom, Torrian is also the founder and lead pastor of Harvest International Church in Southern California, where faith and leadership intersect with community and purpose. He is the visionary behind Masters in the Marketplace and Lions Leading Lions, a bold men's empowerment network helping men restore the roar in life, love, leadership, and legacy.

As a contributing author in Faith, Friendships, and Business, Torrian invites readers to lead from the inside out—with conviction, compassion, and courage. His upcoming book, Focus on Your Five: The Ultimate Guide to Personal and Professional Growth and Transformation, is set to release in Fall 2025.

Through every platform, Torrian lives out his mission: to empower others to lead well, live boldly, and leave a legacy that echoes in eternity.

NOTES

"GOSSIP, N." OXFORD ENGLISH DICTIONARY, OXFORD UP, SEPTEMBER 2024, HTTPS://DOI.ORG/10.1093/OED/5835353428. ACCESSED 3 MAR. 2025.

"PRIDE, N. (1)." OXFORD ENGLISH DICTIONARY, OXFORD UP, DECEMBER 2024, HTTPS://DOI.ORG/10.1093/OED/7380022113. ACCESSED 3 MAR. 2025.

SCRIPTURAL REFERENCES

GENESIS 13:8-9 – LET'S NOT HAVE ANY QUARRELING BETWEEN YOU AND ME...

DEUTERONOMY 31:6 – BE STRONG AND COURAGEOUS... THE LORD YOUR GOD GOES WITH YOU.

DEUTERONOMY 32:11 – LIKE AN EAGLE THAT STIRS UP ITS NEST...

JOSHUA 1:9 – BE STRONG AND COURAGEOUS. DO NOT BE AFRAID...

1 SAMUEL 16:7 – PEOPLE LOOK AT THE OUTWARD APPEARANCE, BUT THE LORD LOOKS AT THE HEART.

2 CHRONICLES 20:22 – THE LORD SET AMBUSHES AGAINST THE MEN OF AMMON AND MOAB...

JOB 8:7 – YOUR BEGINNINGS WILL SEEM HUMBLE, SO PROSPEROUS WILL YOUR FUTURE BE.

PSALM 3:5-6 – I LIE DOWN AND SLEEP; I WAKE AGAIN, BECAUSE THE LORD SUSTAINS ME.

PSALM 34:1 – I WILL BLESS THE LORD AT ALL TIMES...

PSALM 78:4-6 – WE WILL TELL THE NEXT GENERATION THE PRAISEWORTHY DEEDS OF THE LORD...

PSALM 119:105 – YOUR WORD IS A LAMP FOR MY FEET...

PSALM 119:66 – TEACH ME KNOWLEDGE AND GOOD JUDGMENT...

PSALMS 127:3 – CHILDREN ARE A HERITAGE FROM THE LORD...

PSALM 139:23-24 – SEARCH ME, GOD, AND KNOW MY HEART...

PROVERBS 3:15 – SHE IS MORE PRECIOUS THAN RUBIES...

PROVERBS 3:5 – TRUST IN THE LORD WITH ALL YOUR HEART...

PROVERBS 3:5-6 – TRUST IN THE LORD WITH ALL YOUR HEART AND LEAN NOT ON YOUR OWN UNDERSTANDING...

PROVERBS 6:16-19 – THERE ARE SIX THINGS THE LORD HATES...

PROVERBS 8:20-21 – I WALK IN THE WAY OF RIGHTEOUSNESS...

PROVERBS 11:14 – FOR LACK OF GUIDANCE A NATION FALLS...

PROVERBS 14:26 – WHOEVER FEARS THE LORD HAS A SECURE FORTRESS...

PROVERBS 16:11 – HONEST SCALES AND BALANCES BELONG TO THE LORD...

PROVERBS 16:18 – PRIDE GOES BEFORE DESTRUCTION...

PROVERBS 16:3 – COMMIT TO THE LORD WHATEVER YOU DO...

PROVERBS 18:19 – A BROTHER WRONGED IS MORE UNYIELDING THAN A FORTIFIED CITY...

PROVERBS 19:17 – WHOEVER IS KIND TO THE POOR LENDS TO THE LORD...

PROVERBS 27:17 – AS IRON SHARPENS IRON, SO ONE PERSON SHARPENS ANOTHER.

ECCLESIASTES 4:12 – A CORD OF THREE STRANDS IS NOT QUICKLY BROKEN.

ECCLESIASTES 4:9-10 – TWO ARE BETTER THAN ONE... IF EITHER OF THEM FALLS, ONE CAN HELP THE OTHER UP.

ECCLESIASTES 7:11-12 – WISDOM, LIKE AN INHERITANCE, IS A GOOD THING...

ISAIAH 8:10 – DEVISE YOUR STRATEGY, BUT IT WILL BE THWARTED...

ISAIAH 43:2 – WHEN YOU PASS THROUGH THE WATERS, I WILL BE WITH YOU...

ISAIAH 61:3 – TO BESTOW ON THEM A CROWN OF BEAUTY INSTEAD OF ASHES...

JERAMIAH 29:11 – FOR I KNOW THE PLANS I HAVE FOR YOU...

MICAH 6:8 – WHAT DOES THE LORD REQUIRE OF YOU? TO ACT JUSTLY AND TO LOVE MERCY...

MATTHEW 4:1-11 – JESUS WAS LED BY THE SPIRIT INTO THE WILDERNESS TO BE

TEMPTED…

MATTHEW 5:14-16 – YOU ARE THE LIGHT OF THE WORLD…

MATTHEW 5:16 – LET YOUR LIGHT SHINE BEFORE OTHERS…

MATTHEW 5:23 – FIRST GO AND BE RECONCILED TO THEM; THEN COME AND OFFER YOUR GIFT.

MATTHEW 5:44 – LOVE YOUR ENEMIES AND PRAY FOR THOSE WHO PERSECUTE YOU.

MATTHEW 6:26 – LOOK AT THE BIRDS OF THE AIR; THEY DO NOT SOW OR REAP…

MATTHEW 6:33 – SEEK FIRST HIS KINGDOM AND HIS RIGHTEOUSNESS…

MATTHEW 17:20 – IF YOU HAVE FAITH AS SMALL AS A MUSTARD SEED…

MATTHEW 18:35 – THIS IS HOW MY HEAVENLY FATHER WILL TREAT EACH OF YOU UNLESS YOU FORGIVE…

MATTHEW 19:21-35 – SELL YOUR POSSESSIONS AND GIVE TO THE POOR…

MARK 1:35 – VERY EARLY IN THE MORNING… JESUS WENT OFF TO A SOLITARY PLACE, WHERE HE PRAYED.

MARK 8:36 – WHAT GOOD IS IT FOR SOMEONE TO GAIN THE WHOLE WORLD, YET FORFEIT THEIR SOUL?

MARK 10:45 – THE SON OF MAN DID NOT COME TO BE SERVED, BUT TO SERVE…

LUKE 4:1-13 – JESUS, FULL OF THE HOLY SPIRIT, WAS LED INTO THE WILDERNESS…

LUKE 11:9 – ASK AND IT WILL BE GIVEN TO YOU; SEEK AND YOU WILL FIND…

JOHN 3:16 – FOR GOD SO LOVED THE WORLD THAT HE GAVE HIS ONE AND ONLY SON…

JOHN 4:14 – WHOEVER DRINKS THE WATER I GIVE THEM WILL NEVER THIRST…

JOHN 13: 34 – LOVE ONE ANOTHER. AS I HAVE LOVED YOU…

JOHN 16:33 – IN THIS WORLD YOU WILL HAVE TROUBLE. BUT TAKE HEART! I HAVE OVERCOME THE WORLD.

ROMANS 8:28 – IN ALL THINGS GOD WORKS FOR THE GOOD OF THOSE WHO LOVE HIM…

ROMANS 8:37 – IN ALL THESE THINGS WE ARE MORE THAN CONQUERORS…

ROMANS 12:12 – BE JOYFUL IN HOPE, PATIENT IN AFFLICTION, FAITHFUL IN PRAYER.

ROMANS 12:17-19 – DO NOT REPAY ANYONE EVIL FOR EVIL…

1 CORINTHIAN 6:19-20 – YOUR BODY IS A TEMPLE OF THE HOLY SPIRIT...

1 CORINTHIAN 10:13 – GOD IS FAITHFUL; HE WILL NOT LET YOU BE TEMPTED BEYOND WHAT YOU CAN BEAR...

1 CORINTHIAN 10:4-8 – AND DRANK THE SAME SPIRITUAL DRINK; FOR THEY DRANK FROM THE SPIRITUAL ROCK...

2 CORINTHIANS 5:7 – FOR WE LIVE BY FAITH, NOT BY SIGHT.

2 CORINTHIANS 12:9 – MY GRACE IS SUFFICIENT FOR YOU, FOR MY POWER IS MADE PERFECT IN WEAKNESS.

EPHESIANS 2:8 – FOR IT IS BY GRACE YOU HAVE BEEN SAVED, THROUGH FAITH...

EPHESIANS 3:20 – GOD IS ABLE TO DO IMMEASURABLY MORE THAN ALL WE ASK OR IMAGINE...

EPHESIANS 4:15 – SPEAKING THE TRUTH IN LOVE, WE WILL GROW TO BECOME IN EVERY RESPECT THE MATURE BODY...

EPHESIANS 6:16 – TAKE UP THE SHIELD OF FAITH, WITH WHICH YOU CAN EXTINGUISH ALL THE FLAMING ARROWS...

PHILIPPIANS 4:13 – I CAN DO ALL THIS THROUGH HIM WHO GIVES ME STRENGTH.

PHILIPPIANS 4:6 – DO NOT BE ANXIOUS ABOUT ANYTHING...

PHILIPPIANS 4:7 – AND THE PEACE OF GOD... WILL GUARD YOUR HEARTS AND MINDS...

PHILIPPIANS 4:8 – WHATEVER IS TRUE, WHATEVER IS NOBLE... THINK ABOUT SUCH THINGS.

COLOSSIANS 3:17 – WHATEVER YOU DO, DO IT ALL IN THE NAME OF THE LORD JESUS...

COLOSSIANS 3:23 – WORK AT IT WITH ALL YOUR HEART, AS WORKING FOR THE LORD...

COLOSSIANS 4:6 – LET YOUR CONVERSATION BE ALWAYS FULL OF GRACE...

1 THESSALONIANS 5:11 – ENCOURAGE ONE ANOTHER AND BUILD EACH OTHER UP...

HEBREWS 9:14 – CHRIST... OFFERED HIMSELF UNBLEMISHED TO GOD, TO CLEANSE OUR CONSCIENCES...

HEBREWS 11:1 – FAITH IS CONFIDENCE IN WHAT WE HOPE FOR AND ASSURANCE ABOUT WHAT WE DO NOT SEE.

HEBREWS 12:15 – SEE TO IT THAT NO ONE FALLS SHORT OF THE GRACE OF GOD...

JAMES 1:2-3 – CONSIDER IT PURE JOY WHEN YOU FACE TRIALS OF MANY KINDS...

JAMES 1:5 – IF ANY OF YOU LACKS WISDOM, YOU SHOULD ASK GOD...

JAMES 2:17 – FAITH BY ITSELF, IF IT IS NOT ACCOMPANIED BY ACTION, IS DEAD.

JAMES 4:2 – YOU DO NOT HAVE BECAUSE YOU DO NOT ASK GOD.

JAMES 4:6 – GOD OPPOSES THE PROUD BUT SHOWS FAVOR TO THE HUMBLE.

1 PETER 2:9 – YOU ARE A CHOSEN PEOPLE, A ROYAL PRIESTHOOD...

2 PETER 3:9 – THE LORD IS NOT SLOW IN KEEPING HIS PROMISE...

1 JOHN 2:6 – WHOEVER CLAIMS TO LIVE IN HIM MUST LIVE AS JESUS DID.

1 JOHN 4:1 – DO NOT BELIEVE EVERY SPIRIT, BUT TEST THE SPIRITS...

1 JOHN 4:20-21 – WHOEVER CLAIMS TO LOVE GOD YET HATES A BROTHER OR SISTER IS A LIAR...

Made in the USA
Las Vegas, NV
01 June 2025

23002869R00128